Who Will It Hurt When I Die?

Honor Bound  Books

PUBLISHED BY HONOR BOUND BOOKS
7220 Greenhaven Drive, Ste. 7
Sacramento, CA 95831

Library of Congress Cataloguing-in-Publication Data

Goodart, Nan L.
Who Will It Hurt When I Die?[SM]
A Primer on the Living Trust

CIP: 91-076887
ISBN: 09631531-0-2

This publication is intended to provide accurate,
comprehensive information in regard to selected
estate planning topics. It is not meant to be a
substitute for working directly with a qualified
attorney or other estate planning professional, but
rather to help the reader prepare himself for such
work.

This book is sold with the understanding that the
author and the publisher are not engaged in rendering
to the reader any legal, accounting, tax or other
professional services.

Every attempt has been made to assure the accuracy
and completeness of the material contained herein,
but neither the author nor the publisher assumes
liability for any omission or error.

This book is dedicated to all those beautiful people, my clients, who let me inside their lives and their hearts and helped me to see just how much this book was needed.

Acknowledgments

I want to express my love and thanks to the following people:

Glenda Lippmann, who gave her talent, time, skills, creativity and unconditional support to this project. Without her encouragement and insistence my work on this book would never have begun. Because of her support, "If I..." became "When I..." and now it's done! Glenda, thank you for your dedication to excellence (and for always having just the right word)!

David Cawthorn, my editor, who generously did so MUCH more than editing to help me make this book a tangible reality. David, thanks for your unflagging enthusiasm, your brilliance at your work and your unwavering commitment to the quality and success of this book.

Mary Burroughs, my graphic artist. Working with Mary, my question was never: can she create pleasing cover and page designs? It was: how can we choose among them? Thanks Mary for your boundless energy and for bringing your tremendous talent to this project.

Theresa Boschert, for enabling me to take the time off to write with complete assurance that our clients were being well served. Thanks, Theresa, I could not have done it without you.

My staff, Rebecca Burns, Marcia Carpenter, Lynn Fiocchi Kostic and Marilyn Tyrrell, for always being there and doing exactly what I needed done, whether I knew it yet or not! Special thanks to you, Marcia, for keeping the whole office running smoothly and taking such good care of me. Rebecca, Marcia, Lynn and Marilyn—thank you.

Maria Nemeth, whose "You and Money" program got me off the dime and on to bigger things. Thanks, Maria!

Frank Winesett, for his ideas on marketing this book. Thanks, Frank!

Rita Saenz, Patricia Elliott, Ellen Owen, Carl Thompson, Leslie Elgood, Dori O'Rourke, Hunter William Bailey and the many others who supported, encouraged and assisted me in the process. To all of you, thank you!

And finally, Twig, for insisting that I take a play break now and then! Thanks, Twig!

Preface

I have a confession to make regarding the illustrations in this book. With my last name being Goodart you can imagine why it was almost a moral imperative to develop my latent artistic talent. That's how I became a stick figure artist. I'm really quite fond of stick figures. I use them in my seminars and any other place I can get by with it! Both my editor and my graphic artist finally agreed to indulge me and let me use a few to illustrate the text. So now I'm a published artist and I feel quite pleased with myself! I hope you will indulge me also.

But I'm ahead of myself. Let me back up and tell you that I was a high school English teacher for five years and then a college counselor for ten years before I enrolled in law school in 1977. Over 40 years of age before I graduated in 1980, I had plenty of time to experience what it's like to go about the "business" of life without the benefit of a legal education.

When people learn the law at a young age, they seem unaware of how little of the law non-lawyers know or how intimidating the law is to most people. It doesn't seem to occur to them that laypeople often don't even know *what questions to ask!*

I mention this so you will know I truly understand how difficult it can be to get the legal information you need.

That is why in November 1988 I combined my previous training as a teacher with my legal education and began giving monthly public seminars on probate and the revocable living trust.

It had become clear to me by then that people were not being told about the living trust. I began to wonder if the fox wasn't guarding the henhouse. What I mean is, I came to wonder if maybe attorneys were failing to tell their clients about the living trust or were discouraging its use because probating a Will was much more lucrative than drafting a trust.

An article in the prestigious *California Lawyer* magazine published by the State Bar of California confirmed my suspicions. The article made reference to probates having historically been looked upon by attorneys as the source of funding for their retirement.

The scenario goes something like this. Attorneys typically draft a lot of Wills when they first start practicing law. They keep the originals—allegedly as a service to their clients, but in actuality a way to help assure their own employment when the client dies. Later in their career, they move on to a type of law practice more financially rewarding or challenging than estate planning is commonly thought to be. Then, about the time they are ready to scale down their practice, if not retire altogether, the "old" clients start dying, the probates start rolling in, and a high level of income is sustained.

At the date this is written there has been, to my knowledge, no malpractice action filed against an attorney for failure to inform a client of the revocable living trust as an alternative to a Will. That day will come.

However, until that time, those people who not only hear about living trusts, but THE TRUTH about living trusts, should count themselves among the lucky few. It is my intention through my seminars, and now with this book, to enlarge their number!

Nan Goodart
Sacramento, California

Table of Contents

Introduction

Just what IS all the fuss about "living trusts?" How come they are suddenly receiving so much attention? Are they just the latest gimmick being promoted by attorneys on the prowl for new strategies to get our money?

These are questions that people all across our nation are asking, and they deserve answers. You will find those answers here.

Before you can understand "all the fuss," however, you need to have a clear understanding of the court process called probate. I believe that once you do, you will be positively eager to hear about ANY alternative, and the revocable living trust is the best of them!

The cost of probate is one of the reasons you will be interested in the trust. Even if what you own today is the same "stuff" you owned ten years ago, because of inflation alone, it is no doubt worth a lot more now. As a result it would cost a lot more to probate that stuff today.

You see, probate fees are typically based upon the dollar value—the GROSS dollar value—of assets you leave behind. It doesn't take any more work to locate and collect your assets, pay your bills and distribute your estate now than it would have at pre-inflation values, but higher fees are the inevitable result when those fees are based upon the value of your assets.

If you believe legal fees should be based not on the value of your assets, but upon the amount of time it actually takes to wind up your affairs after your death, you want to know about the trust.

If you would want that winding up to take two months rather than two years, you want to know about the trust.

And if you would prefer that the names and addresses of your heirs and the extent of their inheritance did not become a part of public records, where salespeople can (and do) "prospect," then you want to know about the trust.

Before proceeding further, several misconceptions regarding living trusts need to be cleared up. First, if you never heard of living trusts until recently, you may think this is a recent addition to the law. Trusts are, in fact, older than our country. The law of trusts came over on the Mayflower along with other parts of English law.

A second misconception is that trusts are only for the rich. Inflation, if nothing else, has made almost all of us look rich on paper! (Did you ever dream you'd live in a house worth what your's is worth today?!?) Even beyond that, it is my observation that a smaller estate saves more than a large one does with use of the trust. I will explain this in Unit 6.

What happens when you die is not the only reason you will want to know about trusts. As the number of years we can expect to live increases, it is inevitable that more of us will become incapacitated before we die.

If you are like most of my clients, you would rather die than become incapacitated! But how much control do you actually have over this? What you CAN control is how your affairs will be handled if you DO become incapacitated. Again the revocable living trust is the ticket that allows you to by-pass our over-crowded, costly court system.

THIS IS AN AREA OF LAW YOU WANT TO KNOW ABOUT. It is *critical* that you learn about the trust. The costs, delay, and, perhaps most important of all, the *hassle* it can save you and your family will impress you.

This book will provide you with everything you need in order to understand the revocable living trust—what it is, how it works and why YOU might want one.

This is a primer, a basic book for a non-lawyer. It is meant to enlighten you, perhaps even entertain you. Above all, it will empower you to answer a vital question: Who Will It Hurt When I Die?

Some "Housekeeping"

1. Unless otherwise indicated, everywhere in this book that you read the word "trust" it refers specifically to the revocable living trust.

2. I have alternated between masculine and feminine pronouns to avoid the awkward "his or her," "he or she" grammatical constructions. If it appears to you that I have used one more often than the other, please know it was not intentional.

3. Every time the word "Will" is used to refer to the legal document, it will be capitalized in order to avoid confusion.

4. All names have been changed to preserve the privacy of the people upon whose experiences and circumstances I have so gratefully drawn.

5. Finally, a word about the title. I realize there is a grammatical error in it! I know it should be "<u>Whom</u> Will It Hurt When I Die" or even "Who Will <u>Be</u> Hurt When I Die," but neither of those has quite the same 'ring' to my ear, so I left the error!

Now, please, read on!

Always do right. This will gratify some people and astonish the rest.

—Mark Twain

UNIT 1

Your Will:
Better Than Nothing

Just about everybody has heard that they should have a Will. Yet it is estimated only 20-35% of all adults in the United States have signed one.

Some people feel a little superstitious, like maybe signing a Will will bring on their death. For most people it is just a matter of not getting around to it.

After you have read this book, you will understand that a Will is not enough . . . but it IS better than nothing. Here's why.

Lesson 1 ▬▬▬▬▬▬▬▬

Your Will Names Your Beneficiaries

A Will is a document in which you name the people you want to be your beneficiaries—those who will be given something of yours when you die. You may designate particular items as gifts, such as pieces of jewelry or furniture. Or you may give a percentage or the whole of your estate to one person.

"Estate," by the way, refers to everything you own, however little or lot of it there may be. For example, your estate includes your home and any other real estate you own, your furniture, clothing, books, tools, stocks and bonds, life insurance policies, bank accounts and money set aside for retirement.

There are a few states where your Will cannot entirely omit your spouse or your children, but in most states you can give as much or as little as you want to anyone you want to have it, whether they are related to you in any way or not.

Lesson 2 ▬▬▬▬▬▬▬▬

Everyone Has A Will

If you do not sign a Will, your state has a Will for you, based on statutes that vary from state to state.

Typically this Will gives everything to your spouse and/or to your children. Before relying on this Will, however, find out exactly what it provides.

Few married Californians are aware, for instance, that their state's Will for them gives between one-half to two-thirds of all their separately owned property directly to their children! This can create an unintended hardship for the surviving spouse who may, for instance, have been living with his[1] wife in a home separately owned by her. His

---

[1] As I mentioned in the Introduction, I alternate in this book between female and male pronouns rather than using "he or she" and "his or her."

children would now be his landlords and could collect rent on their two-thirds interest...or even evict him.

If any of the children are minors, the situation is even worse. (See Lesson 5 in this Unit for more about this.)

Lesson 3 ▬▬▬▬▬▬▬▬▬▬▬▬▬▬▬▬▬▬

Your Will Nominates Your Executor

"Executor" is the name given to the person nominated in your Will and appointed by the court to wind up your affairs and carry out the wishes you expressed in your Will.[2]

This person will locate all your assets, prepare and file your final income tax return, pay off your creditors, collect the proceeds of any life insurance you carried, close up or sell your business and make the gifts you wanted made at your death. This whole process is called "probate" and Unit 2 is devoted totally to it.

If you do not nominate your own executor, your state's Will names an executor for you. But your state's Will does not waive the posting of a security bond, which is otherwise required. The bond alone can cost multiples of what having your own Will drafted would have cost.

Lesson 4 ▬▬▬▬▬▬▬▬▬▬▬▬▬▬▬▬▬▬

Your Will Nominates A Guardian
For Your Children: Who Will Raise Them?

If any child of yours is a minor (under 18 in most states, under 21 in others) at the time of your death, the court must appoint someone to act as a parent to her. This person will be called the "guardian of her person." This person will finish raising this child, make a home for her and take care of her personal needs.

---

[2]The word "executrix" was used in years past to refer to a female executor. The word is rarely used anymore.

If the child's other natural parent is still living, he is the one the court prefers to appoint as guardian. Your Will, however, can nominate someone you would rather the court appointed. If the other natural parent is either unwilling or unable to act as guardian, then the court will appoint your nominee. On occasion, if good reason is shown, the court will appoint your nominee even if the other parent *is* available and willing.

> **Charlene had taken her little daughter Jill and had moved in with her mother when Jill was two and a half years old. Jill's father, Chuck, rarely came to visit her and rarely even called her. When he did, he was usually high on drugs. Drugs were why Charlene had left Chuck—that, and a suspicion that Chuck was molesting Jill. When Jill was six, Charlene was killed in an auto accident coming home from work. Chuck heard about it and came to get Jill, asserting that, as her father, he was entitled to take her. Charlene's mother had nothing to show the court about Charlene's suspicions or what her preferences would have been and didn't have the money to build a case. Chuck got Jill with no contest.**

Even though the court will have to appoint a guardian whether you nominate one or not, your nomination will prevent this from taking more time than it would otherwise take. This will save your child an extended period of uncertainty and avoid questions she may ask such as: Where will I live now? Who will take care of me? Can I still have my dog? Loss of a child's parent(s) is trauma enough without the child also having to wonder if she will have dinner regularly or sleep in the same place each night.

You can help prevent this, or at least reduce the time it will take, by making your preferences known in a Will.

Lesson 5 ▬▬▬▬▬▬▬▬▬▬

Who Will Manage Your Children's Estate?

"My kid has an estate?" you ask. Well, he may not have one now, but if you die and leave all your "stuff" to him, your estate becomes his estate. Since a minor cannot own property, someone will have to hold and manage it for him until he is "of age." The court will appoint someone to do this. That person will be called the "guardian of his estate."

Even if the child's other parent is available and willing, her petition to be appointed guardian of the child's estate receives no preferential treatment if you have signed a Will nominating someone else. In most states whoever you nominate *will* be appointed unless the court is shown that she is not fit.

The Will your state wrote for you names a guardian for the estate of your children too, but it may not be the person you would have chosen.

> **Jim had divorced Betty, his children's mother, partly because she had no sense of how to manage money. She shopped on impulse and bought far more than they could consume. The family had been bouncing back and forth between days when surplus food spoiled and days when there was no food in the kitchen and no money with which to buy it. Jim died at 36, the victim of a hit-and-run driver. He had never signed a Will. His state's Will named Betty as guardian of his children's estate, so she was appointed by the court. The proceeds of Jim's employer-paid insurance—double indemnity for accidental death—were sent to Betty for her safe-keeping.**

Questions ▬▬▬▬▬▬▬▬▬▬▬▬▬▬▬

Can I write my own Will?

Most of the fifty states allow "holographic" Wills. A holographic Will is one written in your own handwriting. Some states permit no part of a holograph to be typed or printed; some states permit the typing or printing of "nonmaterial" parts. It is safest to handwrite the whole thing.

Like any other Will, the holograph must be dated and signed by you. Most states do not require that anyone witness your signature, and notarizing is not required.

If you are willing to spend some time educating yourself about what a Will should say and how it should (or shouldn't) say it, this is an option you might consider.

You may have seen paralegals advertising they can write a Will for you. Their prices are probably significantly lower than your attorney's. The savings are tempting, and you wonder if that just might be good enough. Well, paralegals are, by definition, people trained *to assist lawyers*. They are not trained to work independently with you.

Now and then someone calls my office to ask what I charge for "just a real simple Will." If price is all they are shopping, they will probably end up in the office of someone other than a lawyer. The outcome can be very unfortunate.

For example, the last non-lawyer drawn Will I read was drafted for a woman in her early thirties, a single parent of two young boys. The paralegal named two people as the boys' co-guardians who not only did not live together, they didn't even live in the same state!

Shared custody is hard enough on children when the child's natural parents are the ones sharing them. This Will went way out of its way to create a ridiculous result.

So beware! An inadequate Will can create more problems than it solves.

Can I put conditions on my gifts?

Any gift can have conditions attached to it, including a gift made at your death.

Some conditions are ones that either can or cannot be met at a specific moment—at the moment of your death, for instance.

Examples are: "If, at the time of my death, my son has graduated from college..." or "If my niece is still single..." or "If my neighbor agrees to adopt my cat...."

At the time of your death, your niece either will be single or she won't. Your neighbor either will agree to adopt your cat or he won't. This kind of condition is easily expressed in a Will.

Another type of condition is one that *may* be met at the time of your death but doesn't *have* to be. For instance, "If my niece has children before she reaches the age of 40..." or "When my son graduates from college..." or "When my granddaughter turns 25...."

For these, something more than just the gift with its condition must be written into your Will. There must also be some "place" created to hold the property while the living wait to see if your niece has children before she turns 40 or if your son graduates from college.

If the condition has only to do with age, and if the age is no more than 25, the gift can be made to what is called a "custodianship," a gift under the Uniform Transfers to Minors Act (UTMA). (More information on UTMA is in the answer to the next question.)

If the condition has to do with anything other than age, such as college graduation, or if the gift is conditioned on an age older than 25, then you will need to have a trust.

You will know a lot about what a trust is and how it works by the time you have finished this book. For now let me say that a trust acts like a receptacle. It holds the property that will be the gift if the condition is met until either the condition is met or the time you allowed for it to be met expires.

This does not mean delaying distribution of other gifts you make in your Will, unless, of course, your Will specifies this. Otherwise your trust will just hold the property you "earmarked" for that beneficiary, safeguarding it until the condition is met—your son graduates from college or the time expires or your niece turns 40 and has not had children. At that time, your gift to your son is completed, or the gift held back for your niece is given instead to the other person you named to be the beneficiary in the event your niece did not meet the condition on her gift.

One final word about conditions on gifts: your condition cannot be "against public policy." What this means is that you cannot, for example, require your beneficiary to commit a crime or to divorce her spouse in order to qualify for your gift.

The bottom line is this: you can place almost any condition you choose on any gift in your Will.

Can I make a gift in my Will to my three-year-old granddaughter?

Part of being a minor is not being able to own anything. So a gift to a minor must be made to an adult who is trusted to hold the minor's gift for her until she becomes an adult— or even later, if you say so.

There are two ways of making this gift in your Will without going into a trust. One is simply to give it to the child outright. However, since a minor cannot own property, this will require that the court step in and name a guardian of the child's estate to hold the gift for her until she is 18, when the guardianship *must* end. Like most court procedures, a guardianship is costly and cumbersome.

An alternative is to direct that your gift be held in a custodianship under the Uniform Transfers to Minors Act

(UTMA) of the state where she lives until your grand-daughter reaches the age you set between 18 and 21 or, in some states, 25. Without a trust, age 25 is the longest a gift can be held back from a beneficiary.

The UTMA is a set of statutes that has been adopted by many states. When a gift is made under UTMA, no court guardianship is required. [You may be familiar with the Uniform Gifts to Minors Act (UGMA); UTMA has replaced it in most states.]

Gifts under UGMA or UTMA are generally preferred to outright gifts. In avoiding the court, the UGMA/UTMA gift saves much time, expense and inconvenience. Of course, if there is no one you would trust to hold your granddaughter's gift for her, scrutiny by the court can be an advantage and a guardianship would be preferred, no matter what it costs or however inconvenient it might be!

One disadvantage of the UGMA/UTMA gift is that it cannot be held any longer than 25. On the other hand, it is better than the guardianship, which must end at 18.

Making an UTMA gift is just a matter of knowing how to write it. It should not add anything to the cost of your Will. This is its advantage over making your gift in trust. Though a gift in trust can go on and on for years, it will almost certainly increase the cost for you.

Do my children have to be given their inheritance as soon as I die if they are not minors?

All gifts in a Will are outright, which means they are given as soon as probate is over, unless the Will hands the gift to a custodian or to a trustee to hold and manage for the beneficiary. A custodian can typically retain the gift until the child is 25. A trustee can retain the gift until any age you specify.

My neighbor says she has a trust in her Will—is that possible?

A trust written into a Will is called a "testamentary" trust. The properly drafted testamentary trust will allow you to retain control of your gift past the time of your death and may save estate taxes *if* it is properly drafted. But it does *not* avoid probate. In fact, in California, it forces an estate into probate that would otherwise escape it! Lesson 1 in Unit 7 examines this more in detail.

To Summarize This Unit ▬▬▬▬▬

In terms of allowing whatever you own when you die to pass to your beneficiaries as quickly, easily, privately and inexpensively as possible, a Will rates less than 1 on an ascending scale of 1-10! But as you have seen, this does not mean that signing your own Will is a completely useless act.

Probate is "a machine which you go into as a pig and come out of as a sausage."

—Adapted from statement of Ambrose Bierce

UNIT 2

Probate:
A Long and Costly Hassle

If you haven't already decided whether or not you want your estate to bypass probate, then I would bet you have not experienced probate. Of those who have, I've yet to meet one who isn't adamant about wanting to avoid it. Maybe this Unit will give you at least a glimmer of what they know that you don't.

Lesson 1 ▰▰▰▰▰▰▰▰▰▰▰▰▰▰▰▰▰▰

What Is Probate?

Whether you sign your own Will or let your state sign one for you, your beneficiaries do not just walk in and take their gifts. Unless you do some planning ahead of time, there will first have to be a probate of your estate. (Remember, "estate" is just a fancy word for the stuff you own.) If you own real estate in more than one state or country, there will probably have to be probates there also.

"Probate" is the name of a court procedure. It did not originate out of a spirit of meanness, but out of a desire to keep an indisputable record of title to land.

"Upon the sacredness of property, civilization itself depends," observed Andrew Carnegie in 1889. That's why keeping accurate ownership records is not a charge to be taken lightly. And it hasn't been taken lightly.

After the founding fathers of our country arrived here, they adopted the very cumbersome procedure that had been developed in England to ensure accurate tracing of land ownership.

England has since streamlined its procedure. Unfortunately, most of our states have not.

In greatly simplified terms, probate calls upon a judge to accomplish the following:

• verify the validity of your Will, if you had signed one; if more than one is found, the judge must decide which one was the last one you signed;

• appoint a person or an institution (such as a bank) to administer your estate, i.e., locate all your assets, pay your debts and wind up your affairs;

• oversee an inventory of your estate and an appraisal of your assets;

• supervise any sale of assets required in order to have enough cash to pay debts, taxes and probate costs;

• require your creditors to prove their claims that you owed them money and set a deadline by which they must present their claims or be forever barred from making them;

• require calculation and payment of any federal and state taxes owed by you on income prior to your death, as well as calculation and payment of any "death taxes" due; and

• see that the gifts you made in your Will are completed to the extent the assets are still in your estate when you die.

One of the reasons probate costs so much is that in most states almost everyone involved in the process works on commission: the executor, the lawyer and the appraiser appointed by the court.

Lesson 2

When Is Probate Necessary?

Probate is necessary any time a person does not plan ahead.

You might say that probate is the "default setting." Like on your home computer, if you do not tell it what to do, it does what it "thinks" most people would want it do to at that point. That's called the "default setting." The law does the same thing; if you don't say what you want to happen when you die, the system "defaults" to probate.

In the absence of your taking preventive action, your estate *will be* probated, unless it is very small.

In California, "very small" means less than $60,000 of total assets or as low as $10,000 in real estate. The amount varies from state to state. Take note that this is a "gross" amount, the fair market value of your assets *before* subtracting *anything* you might owe on any of them. In other words, what your estate would be worth if you owned everything "free and clear." This prevents most people from meeting the requirements of the exception.

Many people avoid probate by holding title to their property as "joint tenants" or by making gifts of their assets while they are still alive. Units 3 and 4 will show how these strategies have *tax* consequences that can cost your beneficiary even more than probate would have—much more, in fact.

What's more, the most these strategies do is *delay* probate. Probate will still be required upon the second death, if joint tenancies and gifts are the extent of the planning co-owners have done.

In some states when the beneficiary was the spouse of the deceased, there is no probate on the first death—at least no probate for what was left *to the surviving spouse*. (This assumes the gift is not left in a testamentary trust—a trust written into a Will. If there is a testamentary trust, the estate will have to be probated even if the beneficiary is the spouse.)

This too only delays probate. Without good planning, the whole estate will still have to be probated when the second one dies.

Lesson 3 ▬▬▬▬▬▬▬▬▬▬▬▬▬▬▬▬

How Much Does Probate Cost?

According to George M. Turner, who has written a well-respected book for attorneys called *Revocable Trusts*, "Expenses in probate expand to consume the money available."

Now that's what I call expensive!

Unfortunately, Mr. Turner knows what he's talking about.

I'm going to walk you through a sample calculation of probate fees, but first I want to state again that probate fees are customarily based on the GROSS value of an asset—its fair market value or what it could sell for. How much may be owing on it does not count. You do not get to subtract the debt.

I suppose the thinking is that it will take the same amount of effort to transfer ownership of something whether there is money owed on it or not. In fact, it may take *more* time if money is owed on it. Of course, it will not necessarily take more time to transfer a home worth $500,000 than a home worth $50,000, but fees have to be based on something, and the gross value of the estate being transferred is the "something" chosen by many states.

Why not just calculate probate fees based on the time actually spent by the attorney? This is almost always an option: to negotiate with the attorney to pay hourly fees instead of the fees provided in the state statutes. But unless the attorney will agree that the statutory fee will be a *cap* on his fees, it is hard to know in advance which way would be better.

If you have hired an attorney recently for anything other than a "flat" fee or a "not to exceed" fee, I would bet I do not need to tell you that attorney's fees can mount up staggeringly fast, whether *or not* you can see it while it is happening.

I was recently staggered by attorney's fees myself.

Having agreed to write a "special needs" trust for clients of that organization called "Estate Planning for the Disabled," I decided to get a general check-up for my basic form of "special needs" trust. I called an attorney well-respected in the community.

"I need some help fairly quickly," I said. "In fact, I need your response within about two weeks."

"Not a problem," she replied.

"Another thing," I said, "there is very little money in this for me—it's almost pro bono (free) work. So I am not interested in paying you a lot to do this."

"I understand," she said.

And so I had my document hand-delivered to her with a cover letter in which I stated the two or three aspects I wanted her to review in the trust. I didn't say this in my letter, but I figured it wouldn't take a tax law specialist like her more than a couple of hours, three at the very most.

I was definitely not asking "exotic" questions.

Instead of the promised two weeks, it took two months for me to get the response I awaited and this after *many* calls, each time reminding her of my urgency. The few callbacks were mainly from an associate, who never did seem to know what it was I wanted to know and who had little time for me anyway, *whatever* it was that I wanted.

As I said, two months later I received a letter addressing not all, but only some of my questions. There was no bill with it. Two more months went by, and still I received no bill. Three months. Four months. I decided that she apparently was not going to bill me, and that maybe this was to be her way of acknowledging and apologizing for how unsatisfactory our work together had been for me.

Five months passed. Six months. Still no bill.

Seven months later here came the bill: $2,802.27!

There was a list of codes representing services, presumably provided to me! No dates were shown. No indication of how much time was spent or by whom. Just a list of codes and a total amount due.

First I was infuriated. Then I was appalled, realizing *most* of her clients must let her get away with a bill like this or she wouldn't send it. It was an unconscionable fee with only the barest of documentation to support it.

A lesson learned firsthand. So, with probate fees, my advice is this: DO NOT sign an hourly fee contract unless the attorney agrees that her hourly fees will not exceed what the statutory fees would have been. Statutory fees may seem high, but at least you know ahead of time what they will be.

So, what WILL they be?

Please go to the **Probate Fee Worksheet** at the end of this Lesson and we'll take this step by step:

1. **Your residence.** What are homes in your neighborhood selling for right now? If you have a pool, a barn, a finished basement or any other valuable feature or improvement, add a low reasonable amount. If your place is smaller or otherwise a little (or a lot) less valuable than the ones that have sold, deduct something for that. Put the figure you came up with on your worksheet. Remember, you do NOT get to deduct any amount you might still owe on it.

I will use a value of $150,000.

Residence   **$150,000**

2. **Furniture and furnishings.** This is the stuff *in* your home, such as your dining room table and chairs, sofa, refrigerator, sheets and towels, pots and pans, china and silver, television and so forth.

For this type of property, estimate what you could sell it all for at a garage sale. I'm going to use $10,000.

Furniture and furnishings   **$10,000**

3. **Vehicles.** Consider what you might get for each vehicle you own if you were to sell it and add those amounts together. Here too, of course, you cannot subtract anything you still owe on any vehicle.

In this category include any boat, travel trailer, motor home or other recreational vehicle you may own.

I'll use $15,000.

Vehicles   **$15,000**

4. **Other personal property.** In this category add up any other non-real estate assets you own. For example, your clothing—not just the furs and other special clothes but also your everyday clothes, your jewelry, your books, tools, hobby inventory, old silver coins, stamp or other special

collections and so forth.

I am going to use $10,000.

Other personal property   **$10,000**

5. **Other real estate.** Here you include a value for any interest you own in any real estate besides your home. Here is where you account for the cabin at the lake, the condominium rental you bought with three friends. If you own a portion of a place, use the value of that portion only. And again, do not subtract what you owe on it.

I am not going to add anything here because most people do not own any real estate other than their home.

Other real estate   **$— 0—**

6. **Cash on hand and in bank accounts.** This includes your checking account, savings account, CDs and market interest accounts, for example; also cash in your safe deposit box, your dresser drawer, your pockets and your fake frozen orange juice can in the freezer.

I'll use the figure $15,000.

Cash   **$15,000**

7. **Investments.** In this category include any stocks you own, any partnership interests, any promissory notes for money you loaned, any bonds—savings, municipal or corporate. I'm going to add $60,000 for investments.

Investments   **$60,000**

8. **Other assets.** Anything you own that is not covered in 1-7 show here. This might include the value of your business, farm equipment, livestock or royalties, to name a few examples.

DO NOT include the value of any retirement accounts or pension plans. DO NOT include the face value of any life insurance.

I am not going to add anything in my sample for "other assets."

Other assets $— 0—

Notice that your debts do not enter into this calculation anywhere.

So here is what I have on my sample:

Residence	**$150,000**
Furniture and furnishings	**10,000**
Vehicles	**15,000**
Other personal property	**10,000**
Other real estate	**— 0—**
Cash	**15,000**
Investments	**60,000**
Other assets	**— 0—**
TOTAL	**$260,000**

Next, let's look at a fee schedule. California's probate fees are about average for our nation, maybe even slightly below average. So I will use California's schedule of fees for executors and attorneys:

8% of	first $15,000
6% of	next $85,000
4% of	$100,001 to $1,000,000
2% of	$1,000,001 to $10,000,000
1% of	$10,000,001 to $25,000,000

A "reasonable amount" for all above $25,000,000.

Now I'll show you how the probate fees would be calculated for my sample estate.

Step 1: Multiply the first $15,000 by 8%. A **$1,200**

Step 2: Multiply the next $85,000 by 6%. B **$5,100**

So far the first $100,000 has been accounted for. If the estate was worth exactly $100,000, the probate fees would be $6,300. Actually, I should say that the probate fees would *begin* there—more about that later.

Step 3: Multiply the balance up to $1,000,000 by 4%. In my sample estate there is $160,000 left after steps 1 and 2.
$160,000 x 4%   C   **$6,400**

Step 4: Multiply any part of the estate between $1,000,000 and $10,000,000 by 2%. My sample estate does not exceed one million, so there will be no figure entered on line D.   D **$—0—**

Step 5: Multiply any part of your estate that is over $10 million by 1%. Here, too, no figure will be entered for the sample estate.
E **$—0—**

Step 6: Add together lines A, B, C, D and E. Put the total on line F.

F **$12,700**

The figure on line F is what the executor and the attorney would split 50-50 for their "ordinary" services if this were a California estate. For "extraordinary" services, they get an additional amount, usually based on their regular hourly fee. "Extraordinary" services include defending against a contest of the Will, preparing any tax returns and selling any property belonging to the estate, even if sale is required in order to pay the "ordinary" fees.

If the executor is also a beneficiary of the estate, he will probably waive his fee. Taking the fee would create an income tax liability for him, while there is no income tax on an inheritance. (There may be "death tax," which will be discussed in Unit 8, but there will be no *income* tax.)

Here is a chart showing a bigger picture of probate fees:

Gross value	Probate fees
$75,000	$4,800
100,000	6,300
150,000	8,300
250,000	12,300
500,000	22,300
1,000,000	42,300
1,500,000	52,300
2,000,000	62,300

It is obvious that the larger the estate, the higher the fees. What is not so obvious, however, is that THE SMALLER THE ESTATE, THE LARGER A PERCENT OF IT will be lost to probate fees.

I have heard people say, "I don't think my estate is large enough to worry about probate fees." The question *really* should be: "Is my estate large enough to NOT worry about probate fees?"

As I said earlier, the fees under the statutory schedule are only where the costs of probate begin; that is the *least* it will cost. There will also be filing fees, publication fees, appraisal fees and so forth. These typically cost hundreds of dollars, not thousands, like the executor's and attorney's fees, but it all adds up. And, of course, "extraordinary fees" are without upward limit.

PROBATE FEE WORKSHEET
(Remember to use gross values!)

Residence	$_____
Furniture and furnishings	$_____
Cars, RVs	$_____
Other personal property	$_____
Other real estate	$_____
Cash on hand and in bank accounts	$_____
Investments	$_____
Other assets	$_____
TOTAL	$_____

Step 1: 8% of first $15,000   A $_____

Step 2: 6% of next $85,000   B $_____

Step 3: 4% of balance up to $1,000,000
4% x $_____   C $_____

Step 4: 2% of balance up to $10,000,000
2% x $_____   D $_____

Step 5: 1% of balance over $10,000,000
1% x $_____   E $_____

Step 6: Total of lines
A, B, C, D and E   F $_____

Line F is what the attorney and executor would be paid to probate your estate today. To this must be added probate referee and appraisal fees, court costs, bonds and "extraordinary" fees.

Lesson 4 ▬▬▬▬▬▬▬▬▬▬▬

How Long Does Probate Take?

One of the main purposes of probate is to assure that all your creditors get paid before your estate is distributed to your beneficiaries. I should say that all your *diligent* creditors get paid; there's more to it than just sending a bill.

Sending a bill is a good start though, because the arrival of the bill will obligate the executor to notify the creditor that more than a bill will be required. Every state sets a limit on how long a creditor can take to present her claim for payment in the form required by the probate court.

In California, creditors have four months which, under certain circumstances, can be extended to almost six months. In some states, creditors have as few as three months.

Once the time has expired, no more claims will be paid.

This is the only built-in delay in probate: the three to six months wait for creditors to present their claims. Despite this, THE AVERAGE PROBATE TAKES MORE THAN TWO YEARS!

You may remember Marilyn Monroe. Her estate was in probate for 18 years!

"Why?" you ask.

Well, some estates are very complicated. The assets are hard to locate, value, sell or divide. Or the beneficiaries are hard to identify or locate. Or there are allegations that the deceased was incompetent when the Will was signed.

The great majority of estates are not all that complicated, however. It is my belief that probates take so long because both the fee and the outcome are all but certain. The attorney is more highly motivated to work on the case that has at least the potential for more money or maybe even less money, but sooner!

Probate is a cumbersome old process that trudges its way to an inevitable conclusion whether the attorney stays "on top of it" or not.

In most cases, a probate *cannot* be completed in much less than nine months. Statistics show it probably *will not* be completed in less than two years.

Lesson 5 ▬▬▬▬▬▬▬▬▬

How Probate Invades Your Privacy

Every paper that gets filed with the court in a probate becomes a matter of public record. This means that *anyone* can go to your county court clerk's office and ask to see your probate file. Not only can they read everything in the file, they can copy it if they wish to. In fact, once they know the number of your probate file, they can request that they be mailed a copy of every paper thereafter placed in your file!

If you remember when movie actress Natalie Wood died unexpectedly, you may also remember how newspapers and magazines reported the details of her possessions—how many fur coats she owned, what they were worth and who would get them.

This information was available because Ms. Wood's estate had to go through probate. A complete inventory of everything she owned, down to the change in her wallet at the time of her death, had to be prepared and filed with the court clerk. And an appraisal of every item had to accompany the inventory.

You may be thinking, "Sure, everyone was interested in Natalie Wood, but who would care about *my* estate?" Well, there are two groups of people who might be very interested in your estate—your friends and neighbors, for one. Salespeople, for another.

Speaking not long ago to a men's service club, I pointed out how some of them may have been lying to their buddies for years, letting on as if they owned a lot more and owed a lot less than was true. If their estate has to go through probate, their secret most definitely will *not* go to their graves with them!

Now, you may not have been spinning tales at all. You may just prefer that your business *stay* your business. The truth is it will become everybody's business if you let your estate go through probate.

Salespeople regularly comb probate files for prospects. It is like shooting fish in a barrel for them. Your file, in addition to containing the inventory and appraisal of your estate, will provide the names *and addresses* of your beneficiaries and show what part of your estate each one will be receiving. You can see the advantage a salesperson would have in knowing ahead of time that the person she is talking to will soon be coming into an inheritance.

Questions

Is probate ever desirable?

Most people feel intense scrutiny of their estate and its distribution would not be necessary. But it can, in some cases, be very important. Consider the case where the one named to administer the estate does not like someone named as a beneficiary. If that administrator will be accountable to the court, the beneficiary may be more likely to receive her gift...all of it! Otherwise, who knows?

Additionally, probate sets a definite ending to the time period during which your creditors can file claims. If your particular estate is one that may owe money to people not likely to receive news of your death very quickly— creditors in other countries, or even other states, for instance— probate lets the risk be theirs. Otherwise, the beneficiaries bear the risk that a tardy creditor will appear.

This is not a risk without end, however. In California, creditor claims not barred by probate can be made only within the 12 months following the death of the debtor.

Probate is not without merit. In fact, it can be totally necessary and appropriate for an estate. The problem with probate arises out of the fact that, although only a handful of estates will have far-flung creditors or administrators whose integrity may falter and whose actions may need intense scrutiny, almost all estates are subjected to it anyway.

Do I have to hire an attorney?

Theoretically, you do not have to hire an attorney. But probate is a rather complex procedure. Probate courts have about one quarter the time they really need to give each case its due. As a result, probate judges may not be of much assistance when someone who doesn't know much about what she is doing is representing an estate in court.

I suppose it could be said that you do not have to hire an attorney as long as you have high tolerance for impatience, abruptness and embarrassment.

What happens if I only own a part interest in a piece of property?

If you own the property as a joint tenant, your interest in it goes to your surviving co-owner without probate. Joint tenancy can create even more expensive problems, however, as you will see in Unit 4.

Otherwise, what goes through probate is just the portion of the property that you owned.

How about property I own out of state?

If the property is real estate, then there will probably have to be a probate in that state as well as one in the state where you lived.

I've signed a power of attorney. Won't my estate avoid probate?

A power of attorney—even a "durable" power of attorney—expires when you do. It has absolutely no effect once you have died.

To Summarize This Unit ▬▬▬▬▬

Probate is an expensive and invasive court procedure that most estates will undergo, whether they need it or not, unless good estate planning has been done.

How To Avoid Probate:
An Overview

As you have learned, probate is a very costly, time-consuming hassle. In that way, it is not unlike many procedures established for the benefit of people who do not take enough responsibility for some aspects of their lives.

I am thinking, for instance, about the driver's license renewal process here in California. If a person is willing to handle this matter a little ahead of time, it can be accomplished by mail. The person who waits until her license expires must wait and wait in line to get a new one. It's no more costly, in this case, but a time-consuming hassle? You know it.

Neither probate nor in-person license renewal is the *preferred* way of accomplishing the task. Both are "default settings." They are just how you have to do it if you never got around to doing it the easy way.

In the case of probate, there are several ways of avoiding it. Not all of them are good. In fact, some of them are worse than probate!

Four probate-avoiding strategies will be considered in detail in the next four units. They are: (1) reducing your estate by making gifts *before* you die; (2) holding title in a way that automatically gives your share of an asset to your co-owners at your death; (3) signing a contract where you can name a beneficiary, such as a life insurance policy; and (4) creating a "living" trust.

In addition to these four primary options there are a couple of others that need to be mentioned. One is: don't acquire an estate—aptly stated in one of Bob Dylan's songs that "when you have nothing, you have nothing to lose." The other is: marry someone and leave everything you own to him. While this will avoid probate of *your* assets in most states, it restricts your choice of beneficiaries. In addition, it depends upon you being the first to die. What's more, it does nothing to eliminate probate of your spouse's estate, which will cost even more than it would have because now your spouse has not only all his stuff but yours too!

As I said, some of the ways to avoid probate are worse than probate. That's why you need to be knowledgeable about each one.

By the way, avoiding probate does not mean all the

steps of the procedure are avoided. In fact, most of them are still necessary. Your debts, as well as your taxes, still have to be paid. Your assets should still be appraised (see Unit 9, Lesson 2 for the reasons). The gifts you wanted made will still have to be delivered. The difference is all these things will be done without the scrutiny of the probate court and the cost, delay and hassle that accompany that.

Experience is the name everyone gives to their mistakes.

— Oscar Wilde

UNIT 3

Avoiding Probate
With Lifetime Gifts

Giving away your assets during your lifetime is a way of avoiding probate at your death. But you will learn in this Unit how this strategy can backfire.

Lesson 1 ▬▬▬▬▬▬▬▬▬▬▬▬▬▬

The Cost Of A Gift #1

More than once someone in my seminar audience has been inspired to say: "I'll take care of that—I'll just give it all away!" And, of course, it's true. If you do not own anything when you die, nothing will have to go through probate.

However, this can be a classic case of "out of the frying pan, into the fire!" Your wanting to avoid probate does not necessarily mean you no longer want your assets. The result of your making a gift, understandably, is that you no longer have it for *yourself!* You lose all use, benefit and control over whatever you give away.

> **An older gentleman told me he had decided to start giving some of his stock in a local bank to his granddaughter. Grandad had been accumulating this stock for years. Whenever he heard someone wanted to sell, he would buy. The stock had appreciated a lot over the years and Grandad's estate, as well as his self-esteem, were bolstered by the success and promise of this investment and the power he held as a major shareholder. The next time I spoke to Grandad he told me sadly that his granddaughter had sold the stock he gave her to buy herself a new car. Naturally, he had discontinued his gifting program.**

In my years of practice I have had very few clients—maybe five or six in all—who felt absolutely certain they would never in their lifetimes want or need some relatively substantial portion of their assets. (If it is *not* "substantial," then giving it away may not make enough difference to bother making the gift.)

In these days of living longer but not necessarily better, most of us have known of at least one family whose resources were rapidly dwindling and who were on the threshold of applying for public benefits for Mom.

The good news is that public benefits exist; the bad news is that they do not cover the level of care Mom may be used to and you want her to have. Medicaid's idea of dentistry, for example, is to pull a troublesome tooth instead of repairing it.

The point is that not many of us are willing to just give away very much of whatever we have managed to accumulate, however large or small it may be. That's why probate can be inexpensive compared to the cost of "just giving it all away."

> **Barbara's uncle Horace had been a widower for many years. His eyesight was failing now, and he didn't know how much longer he would be able to live in his own home. However, he wanted to be sure that Barbara would get his house when he died. So Horace signed a deed giving the house to Barbara. Then he called her and asked her to come over.**
>
> **Horace explained to Barbara that he wanted her to have his house, but he wanted her assurance that he could go on living there as long as he was able. He also wanted her to take care of paying the taxes and insurance. He would give her the money, but he wanted her to write the checks and be sure everything got paid on time. Barbara agreed, and Horace gave her the deed he had signed.**
>
> **When I met Barbara it was four years later. Horace was still able to live alone and was**

doing fine. A big problem had arisen at her end of the bargain, though. She and her husband were divorcing, and her husband had declared bankruptcy. The couple owed far more than they could pay. Creditors, of course, were demanding information about everything they owned. Barbara's question to me was: "Do I have to tell them about Horace's house?"

"Yes," I told her, "you do."

Barbara may well end up unable to keep her agreement with Horace. It looks like what is now Barbara's house may be sold out from underneath him.

Horace had thought that, by making a separate agreement with Barbara, he was avoiding the "hard part" of giving away his house. Who could have guessed it would have come to this?

Lesson 2 ▬▬▬▬▬▬▬▬▬▬▬▬▬▬

The "Wrong One" May Die First!

Something else can go awry with a gifting program: the "wrong one" may die first.

One family I worked with several years ago owned acres and acres of what had been farmland but had become prime residential property. Dad had died some years before, leaving Mom half his share and his son, Alan— an only child in his early 50s—the other half.

> **Mom was absolutely convinced that her best strategy would be to get all the property into Alan's name. She would hear nothing to the contrary. So the gifting was accomplished. Less than a year later, Alan went on vacation and fell dead of a massive heart attack in his hotel room. Mom got all the property back—minus the very considerable costs of probate and estate taxes, of course.**

If you are like most parents, chances are you discount totally the fact that your children could predecease you.

But, of course, the fact is they may die in an accident or of some unexpected, natural cause. The solution is to diversify and not let your planning be based on only one set of assumptions.

Lesson 3 ▬▬▬▬▬▬▬▬▬▬
The Cost Of A Gift #2

In October 1989 the newspaper reported a story out of Bennington, Vermont, about a woman in her 90s who loaned her grandnephew money to buy a car. Less than a month later he wrapped the car around a tree and a passenger was paralyzed from the waist down. The passenger sued the woman, saying she was negligent in lending grandnephew the money. A jury awarded him $950,000!

The jury would have probably reached its verdict even sooner than it did had she made a *gift* of the money to buy the car.

My point is, be aware of the liability the giver can acquire upon making a gift of assets. A *whole lot* of assets could have been probated for $950,000! Remember Uncle Horace in Lesson 1? He had no way of knowing what the future held for the financial health of his donee. His "reversal of fortune" could be yours as well if you're not careful.

Lesson 4 ▬▬▬▬▬▬▬▬▬▬▬▬▬▬

"Just Adding A Name" Is Still A Gift

If you do not pay your bills, your creditors can come after you and sue you for payment. With certain exceptions they can force sale of your assets if cash is not otherwise available.

Adding someone else's name on your assets makes your assets part of the things your "someone else" owns when *his* creditors go looking for something to attach.

To be sure, "just adding a name" doesn't appear to be as big a step as giving the property away altogether. Giving your son the house feels a whole lot different than adding his name to yours on the title. And yet the results are the same in many ways.

As you saw in Lesson 1, you acquire the liabilities of the one whose name you put on your assets, even if you just add his name to yours.

If you decided to sell your property, "someone else's" signature will be required. Also, he can cloud your title to real estate with "wild" deeds. In fact, he could force you to buy him out, or he could sell his interest in your house to someone else. As a result, you have lost control.

"Just adding a name" does not necessarily avoid probate anyway.

If title is held in joint tenancy, the property will avoid probate. Otherwise, the portion of ownership that you kept will still have to be probated. This gift too can cost more than probate and create more worry about liability and loss of control. At least the cost of probate is only money and time.

Joint tenancy creates its own problems, as you will see in Unit 4.

Lesson 5 ▬▬▬▬▬▬▬▬▬▬▬▬

The Cost Of A Gift #3

There is another unwelcome result of lifetime giving. A lifetime gift deprives your beneficiary of a "stepped-up basis." In other words, if your gift is something that has increased in value since you bought it, your beneficiary will lose more to income taxes when she sells it than she will if you let her inherit it from you.

To put it another way, if you put your children's names on your property while you are alive, when they sell that property, they will have to subtract *what you paid* for the property to calculate the amount of income tax they will owe.

However, if the children receive that same property from you upon your death, then when they sell it, they will subtract *what the property was worth at the time of your death* to calculate the amount of income tax they will owe.

A client of mine is retired from Proctor & Gamble. Over his years of employment there he acquired a substantial amount of stock in the company. He paid an average of $8 a share. On the day of our first meeting, the stock was selling for $108 per share!

If he gives this stock to his children now, which is what he came in to ask about, they will have to pay income tax on the difference between $8 and the selling price. So if they sell the stock for $120 per share, they will pay income tax on $112 per share. At a 28 percent rate, federal income tax would be $31.30 per share.

If he lets his children receive this stock as an inheritance, they will pay tax only on the difference between its value at his death and the price for which they sell it. For instance, if they sell it for $120 and it was worth $108 when they inherited it, they will pay income tax only on $12 per share! At 28 percent that would be $3.36—in this case, only about a tenth of what their tax would be the other way.

Questions

Should I even take my daughter's name off my bank accounts?

I've often heard a person say, "I only put my daughter's name on my account so she could get to my money should I have an emergency."

Well, there is a better way to accomplish this, a way that carries with it no risk of losing *your* money to *her* creditors. That way is a "power of attorney."

A power of attorney is a document that lets you designate someone, called your "agent," to take action for you if you are unable or unavailable to take action for yourself. In this way, your daughter acquires access to your assets *without any ownership*. The extent of her power is to use your assets only to pay your debts and to meet your needs.

Most banks have their own form of power of attorney they want you to sign. You need to verify there is no conflict between your general power of attorney and the bank's form. Barring that, it is appropriate for you to sign both.

You will find more information about powers of attorney in Unit 10, which is entirely devoted to these absolutely essential documents.

Can I keep a "life estate" if I make a gift?

A "life estate" refers to a right to continue using whatever you are giving away for as long as you live. The gift won't have much, if any, effect until you die.

You saw in Lesson 1 where Horace attempted to retain a life estate. He would have fared better had he put his life estate on record by writing it into the deed he gave Barbara.

So, yes, you can keep a life estate. But, in my experience, it is not merely the right to go on occupying the house, for example, that has value to the owner. The equity in it may provide financial security and may even be a source of income.

Plus there is pride in ownership. The home may be the only—or at least the primary—asset a person feels he has to show for a lifetime of work.

Today's elders lived through the Great Depression when many, many people lost their homes. For them, owning a home may provide them with assurance of their survival.

All of these factors need to be considered, all the while bearing in mind that there are other ways to avoid probate that don't remotely affect a person's financial security, sense of success or self esteem at all.

To Summarize This Unit ▰▰▰▰▰▰

Any assets you give away during your lifetime will not be part of your estate when you die. So they will not have to be probated. Certain tax results, however, could make this strategy cost much more than probate. As for other results, such as loss of use, loss of control and liability exposure, the cost may not be measurable, but it can be just as devastating.

If you do not define the terms of your own existence,
someone else will do it for you.

—Unknown

UNIT 4

Avoiding Probate
With Joint Tenancy

Joint tenancy is a form of co-ownership of property. It is a way to hold title when more than one person owns the property. Being joint tenants means the survivor of you automatically ends up owning the whole property. This is how joint tenancy avoids probate.

Lesson 1 ▬▬▬▬▬▬▬▬▬▬▬▬

The Right To Name Your Beneficiary Is Lost

The result of holding title in joint tenancy is that, when the first joint tenant dies, her share goes *automatically* to the surviving joint tenant(s). If there were three co-owners, the surviving two would each then own one-half. When the second joint tenant dies, the survivor will be sole owner of the property, regardless of anything stated in a Will. The property is out of the estate before the Will is out of the safe deposit box.

This is not always what people intend. Here's a good example:

Many years ago, Mark's mother put her two children, Mark and Jim, on the deed to her house as joint tenants with herself. When mother passed on, Mark and Jim each became half owners of the property as they each acquired half of mother's one-third interest (joint tenants always have only *equal* shares). They left title in joint tenancy.

Since mother died Mark has put out money, unmatched by his brother, to maintain and improve the property, thinking all the while that it would be a valuable inheritance for his children.

Mark was shocked to learn that, as title stood, ownership of his half of the property would automatically go to Jim if Mark died first. Conversely, of course, Mark would become sole owner if his brother died first, but that did not make the risk of "losing" it all acceptable to him.

Automatic transfer of ownership to your co-owners may not be what you have in mind at all.

Lesson 2

Bad News For Married Joint Tenants

All most people know about joint tenancy is that it avoids probate. That's why, often on the advice of their real estate agent, they quickly opt for joint tenancy.

Many states don't even require probate of assets that are passing at death from one spouse to the other. California, for instance, requires no probate at the first death.

However, even if you live in a state which requires probate between spouses, you might still choose probate over the tax result of owning property with your spouse as joint tenants.

Here is why.

If you hold title to your property as community property,[3] then when the first spouse dies, *all of the appreciation that has occurred since you purchased the property is "forgiven"* for income tax purposes.

If title was held in joint tenancy, only one-half of the appreciation is forgiven. This can mean thousands, if not tens of thousands, of dollars difference.

> **Clara and Harry own a small duplex. They paid $40,000 for it many years ago. The property is now worth $160,000, an increase in value (the "appreciation") of $120,000.**
>
> **If Harry and Clara sell this property now, while both are alive, there will be income tax due on the appreciation of $120,000. At 28**

---

[3] Nine states are currently community property states: Arizona, California, Idaho, Louisiana, Nevada, New Mexico, Texas, Washington and Wisconsin.

percent, the rate most of us pay, they would owe the IRS $33,600 plus whatever tax their state collects on income.

If Harry dies and then Clara sells, how much she will owe the IRS depends on how they held title at the time Harry died.

If they held title as joint tenants, Clara won't owe any tax on the half of the appreciation that "belonged" to Harry. But she will owe tax on her half of the appreciation. Her half of the appreciation is $60,000. At 28 percent she would owe the IRS $16,800.

However, if Clara and Harry held title to the duplex as community property, Clara will not owe the IRS *any* tax on the appreciation—not now and not later! (This is called a "full step-up in basis.")

So here you see that husband and wife joint tenants end up paying many thousands of dollars in income tax in order to avoid a procedure they would have avoided anyway.

The costs of probate never approach income tax rates. So even if the property *did* have to be probated, that probate would have cost Clara considerably less than the income taxes due the other way.

Lesson 3

Bad News For Unmarried Co-Owners

Joint tenancy is also a thorn in the rose bush of co-ownership for people not married to each other. The Internal Revenue Code[4] singles them out for special treatment.

[4]Section 2040(a)

The first to die will be presumed to have paid for the whole property. Therefore, the whole value of it will be included in her estate when calculating the estate taxes due.

The potential here, of course, is double taxation. The whole value is in the first estate as well as in the second estate.

The presumption can be overcome by detailed records showing each individual's equal contribution toward purchase and all other expenses, such as maintenance, repairs and improvements. If all payments are made out of a joint bank account, you must be able to trace the contributions to the account. It certainly can be done. The question is: will you do it?

Here again we have a probate avoidance strategy that can cost many times what probate would cost.

Lesson 4

Bad News For The Heirs Of The First One To Die

In my experience, spouses rarely want to place any restrictions on the survivor's use of whatever they own together when the first one dies. But I find they often want to direct who will get whatever might be left of it when the survivor dies. This isn't of as much concern to a couple with their own children. However, with blended families, comprised of his children, her children and sometimes *their* children, this issue can be of vital concern.

I notice that wives worry about remarriage of their husbands much more than vice versa. She just *knows* he will remarry, and she may even think she knows who the new wife will be. She worries about *her* kids, even about *their* kids "losing out" to a surviving stepmother or having to share with a blended family. She wants to feel some degree of certainty that only her kids, not the new wife and not somebody else's kids, will get what had been hers.

No such certainty is possible in joint tenancy.

When property passes from one person to another by joint tenancy, it is a "no strings attached" type of gift. The survivor alone controls who gets what's left when he dies. The heirs of whoever dies first are out of luck.

This result can be totally avoided with a trust.

Lesson 5

The Lost "Death Tax" Exemption

You will know more about "death taxes" after you have read Unit 8, but for now let me share this. At the time this is written, each of us has a credit against death taxes that covers $600,000 worth of assets.

If your beneficiary is your spouse and she survives you, you will not use your credit at that time. This is because any amount of assets can pass to a spouse free of death tax.

If your property passes to your spouse through joint tenancy, however, your credit is lost forever. Though not used upon your death, joint tenancy eliminates the possibility of preserving your credit for use when the survivor dies and the assets pass to whoever comes next.

With a trust, both credits can be preserved for use upon the second death. How this works is discussed in detail in Unit 9. The bottom line is that this enables a "death tax" savings of up to $235,000, all lost with joint tenancy.

Lesson 6

A Few Leftovers

1. Joint tenancy only avoids the *first* probate. The estate will still have to be probated on the second death unless the survivor does some better planning than he did when both of them were alive.

2. If the joint tenants die in the same accident, usually each is treated as if he or she had been the survivor. Right— *two* probates.

3. Adding someone's name as a joint tenant on your property brings with it the exposure to liability that is discussed in Unit 3, Lesson 4.

Questions ▆▆▆▆▆▆▆▆▆▆▆▆▆▆▆▆▆▆▆▆▆▆▆

Is joint tenancy ever appropriate?

Joint tenancy can be used in the following situation:

Property that is not likely to enjoy much, if any, appreciation and was paid for by two or more people, equally, who would be each other's choice of beneficiary anyway, but are not married to each other.

First of all, you have seen in Lesson 2 how joint tenancy exposes appreciation to income taxation. This need not concern you if the property is not likely to appreciate in value. For example, look at a bank account. While it may grow, its growth will typically not be dramatic. Another example is an automobile, which is more likely to decrease in value than appreciate.

Second, if the property was in fact jointly purchased— both or all of you put up the purchase money *equally*, are all on the loan, have equally shared all expenses *and* have the records to prove it—then you are not exposing your property to attachment or collection by the creditors of someone who has no actual financial interest in the property.

Third, if you are not married to each other, you will not be losing out on the tax savings discussed in Lesson 2.

In this situation, joint tenancy need not be ruled out.

How can I tell if we are joint tenants?

For property to be owned as joint tenants, the ownership document has to *say* "joint tenants" or some variation such as these: JT, JTWROS (with right of survivorship), or Jt Ten.

By "ownership document" I mean a deed (real estate), a "pink slip" (automobile), a promissory note evidencing a debt owed *to* you. Unless there is *something* after your names that means "joint tenancy," you do not hold the property as joint tenants.

If you live in a "separate property" state (as opposed to a community property state), you need to know that a "tenancy by the entirety" is a form of joint tenancy.

What if we are joint tenants—can that be changed?

The form of your co-ownership is easily changed. For real estate, it can be accomplished by signing a deed from yourselves as joint tenants to yourselves as tenants in common or community property or however you want it. For other types of property, such as a bank certificate of deposit (CD), go to the bank and amend the ownership document (the certificate).

Simpler yet is for you and your co-owner to sign one written agreement which states that, regardless of what existing ownership documents may say, all co-owned assets are held by you as whatever-you-prefer. And then you must remember next time you acquire an asset to take title the "right" way.

To Summarize This Unit ▬▬▬▬

Holding title to your co-owned assets as "joint tenants" allows those assets to bypass the probate process. However, the *tax* results of your property passing in joint tenancy can be many times the cost of probate.

In addition to the cost is the loss of all control, if you are the first co-owner to die, along with the impossibility of preserving the death tax exemption of the first to die.

This is a case of the cure being worse than the condition.

The problem of our age is the proper administration of wealth.

—Andrew Carnegie

UNIT 5

Avoiding Probate By Contract

What you have seen so far are ways of avoiding probate that can cost, not only more than probate, but *many* times more than probate.

In this Unit you will look at ways of avoiding probate that have very little drawback or disadvantage.

Lesson 1 ▬▬▬▬▬▬▬▬▬▬▬▬▬▬▬▬

ATF, ITF and POD Accounts

An ATF account is an account at a bank, credit union or savings and loan on which you have named a beneficiary. This will appear in your "contract" with the bank—those signature cards you filled out when you opened the account. Most signature cards have a box you can check to show you are naming a beneficiary for that account.

ATF means "as trustee for." These are also known as POD accounts—"pay on death"— and ITF accounts—"in trust for."

This is an informal "trust" arrangement. As you will see in Unit 6, the law allows any property held "in trust," even an informal trust, to bypass the aged and cumbersome probate process.

An ATF account is not a substitute for a trust—it IS a form of trust available only for bank accounts and a very limited number of other similar assets.

Whoever is named will receive everything in your ATF account when you die no matter to whom your Will might give it. This overrides your Will (and your "formal" trust as well if you have one).

If you decide to have a formal trust, one that can hold ALL your assets, you do not need to use an ATF account. But if you decide that you will not have a formal trust, be sure to take full advantage of an ATF account to avoid probate.

If the beneficiary you want to name is a minor, verify with an attorney how best to express your ATF gift.

In California—and other states that have adopted the Uniform Transfers to Minors Act—naming someone as "custodian" for your beneficiary assures there will be no necessity of a court guardianship. Again, check with a local attorney about the best way to handle this in your state or you could simply be replacing one court procedure (probate) with another (guardianship)!

Lesson 2

Life Insurance

You always have the opportunity to name a beneficiary on any life insurance policy you own. That is one of the privileges of owning the policy.

Sometimes you are given the opportunity to name the beneficiary of a policy owned by someone else, such as your employer.

Always take that opportunity!

When I got my first teaching job, I went as directed to the personnel office to fill out some forms. One form was used to name a beneficiary of the life insurance the school district provided me as an employee benefit. Another was a beneficiary designation for the money that would be accumulating in my state teachers' retirement account.

When I expressed some uncertainty about filling these out, the person at the counter told me, "Oh, just put 'my estate' in there. That's what everyone else does."

Almost 20 years later in law school, I learned what a costly piece of free advice that could have been! You see, your retirement money does not usually have to go through probate and neither do the proceeds of your life insurance, UNLESS you have named "my estate" as your beneficiary! That forces it into probate! Verify that you have not made this mistake.

Speaking of beneficiary designation forms, read the fine print. Almost every one I have read provides that, if any of the beneficiaries you have named die before you do, those *who survive you* split the proceeds.

My experience with hundreds and hundreds of families is that most of them want the children of a beneficiary who predeceases them to have that beneficiary's share. If one of their three sons dies before they do, for instance, then they want that son's children—their grandchildren—to have that son's share.

If the pre-printed instruction does not reflect your preferences, line it out on the form and *write in* how you want it to be.

Lesson 3 ▬▬▬▬▬▬▬▬▬▬▬▬▬▬

Retirement Accounts, Pension Plans, Deferred Compensation, Tax-Sheltered Annuities

Retirement accounts and pension plans of all kinds, deferred compensation accounts and TSAs come with a built-in probate avoidance feature. You are usually invited to name a beneficiary as part of the "set up" process, and you should always do so.

As with life insurance, always name one or more persons or charities or other institutions. Do NOT leave it blank or write "my estate" or "my executor."

This is so easy and so important that I suggest you write or call today for a copy of all your currently effective beneficiary designations to verify you have named appropriate beneficiaries. For many, many people, these assets constitute the bulk of their estate. How unfortunate it would be if they had to be probated.

At the start of this Unit, I said that avoiding probate by contract (such as a contract with your bank, your life insurance company or the trustee of your IRA) has very little drawback. That implies there is *some* degree of drawback. In fact, there is.

If you were to become incapacitated and had done no more estate planning than naming a beneficiary on your accounts, there would be no structure in place for you to avoid the court procedure called "conservatorship."[5]

In brief, a conservatorship is very similar to probate. You go through inventories, appraisals, accountings, court

---

[5] Some states use the term "guardianship" for both minors and adults. Other states distinguish between the procedures by calling it a "conservatorship" when the incompetent person is an adult.

investigations, petitions for orders and so forth, only this one will go on as long as you live! Also like probate, a conservatorship is costly. Unit 10 addresses the conservatorship in detail and looks at your alternatives.

There is another drawback to letting the naming of beneficiaries on your accounts be the extent of your estate planning. There will be no structure in place to manage that gift in the event that your beneficiary is either a minor or incapacitated herself.

Or if your spouse or your parent is your beneficiary and she is receiving any public benefits at the time of your death, such as Medicaid for example, this does not protect your gift from having to be "spent down."

Unlike the previous alternatives to probate—lifetime gifting and joint tenancy—at least this one doesn't make anything worse! It may not be perfect, but it's not going to hurt you!

Questions ▰▰▰▰▰▰▰▰▰▰▰▰▰

If the beneficiary I name on my savings account is a minor, will the credit union hold it for him until he turns 18?

No, your credit union would have no authority to keep your money. Someone would have to petition the court to name a guardian for the minor. Once appointed, the guardian could choose to leave the funds at that credit union, but only the court, through the guardian, can control a minor's assets. (Unless, of course, you have planned well and have named a custodian to hold the minor's inheritance. See the Questions in Unit 1 for more information on the Uniform Transfers to Minor Act.)

If I create a trust naming my beneficiaries, does that revoke the beneficiary designations I made at the bank?

No, it does not. The beneficiary you named on your bank accounts, life insurance and retirement accounts is not affected by your trust (or your Will). These "direct" designations override all others.

Wouldn't it be simpler if I just named one of my children as beneficiary and told her that I expect her to split it with her brothers and sisters? They don't leave you much room on those forms.

It would be simpler because it is simpler to write one name than three or four—or even two! But once the proceeds are paid to that child, they are hers. What happens to them after that is strictly up to her.

Even if she honors your wishes and gives everyone his fair share, this can create gift tax problems for her because now it isn't *you* making the gift but *her*.

Another problem has arisen when the one who received the whole proceeds of the life insurance died before getting the money divided up and handed out. Since it all came to her alone, it was all part of her estate when she died, and so it legally belonged to *her* heirs alone. You can see how this could get very complicated.

The best way to identify your beneficiaries is to name each one of them *and* say what you want to happen to the shares of any of them who do not survive you.

To Summarize This Unit ▬▬▬▬

Certain types of assets give you the option of naming a beneficiary at the time you acquire them. Examples are bank accounts, life insurance policies and retirement accounts, including IRAs. In essence, you can say, "When I die, give everything then held in this account to (beneficiary you name)."

Always take advantage of this opportunity. Take the time to verify that all your accounts have a beneficiary named and that the beneficiary named would still be your choice.

Once you have created a trust, you can have all your accounts and policies paid to it at your death. Then all your assets can benefit from the good estate planning that is reflected in your trust. Until then, take full advantage of ATF accounts.

Put not your trust in money, but put your money in trust.

—Oliver Wendell Holmes

UNIT **6**

Avoiding Probate With A Trust:
The Revocable Living Trust

F inally we come to the revocable living trust as an alternative to probate—the flawless alternative!

As you have seen, the other ways to avoid probate all have a cost. Basically, you have to give up control of your assets or give up the income and use of your assets or both!

The revocable living trust allows you to avoid probate and reduce, if not eliminate, death taxes while *retaining* full control and use of your assets.

Lesson 1 ▬▬▬▬▬▬▬▬▬▬

Defining The "Revocable Living Trust"

A. "Trust"

There are verbal definitions of what a trust is, of course, but I have found that this simple picture explains it better than anything else:

Illustration 6-1

The person on the left and the person on the right are both holding apples.

The person on the left holds his apple in his hand. The person on the right holds his apple in a basket.

A TRUST IS JUST LIKE THAT BASKET.

"In trust" is just another way of holding your assets— of holding title to your assets—just like a basket is a way of holding an apple.

B. "Revocable" Trust

The word "revocable" retains its usual meaning: capable of being revoked, cancelled, rescinded or repealed. You can change just a part of your revocable trust or you can get rid of it altogether.

Revoking a revocable trust is like cutting the bottom out of a basket. Everything in it comes tumbling out onto your lap and is just like it was before.

Each time I say "trust" in this book I mean a revocable trust unless I say otherwise at the time.

Some trusts are irrevocable. When property is transferred to an irrevocable trust, it is like giving it away. In fact, it *is* giving it away! The giver loses the control of the asset as well as its income, use and benefit. It is no longer something she owns; it belongs to someone else now. This can result in certain tax savings. But in my experience there are just not a whole lot of people who feel so sure they have more than they will ever need that they are willing to give away part of it now.

There is one kind of irrevocable trust people with estate tax worries should know about, however. It works a little bit differently in that it creates its own asset. This particular irrevocable trust is commonly called a "life insurance trust." You make gifts of money to it, and the trustee uses the money to pay the premiums on a policy insuring your life.

When you die, there will be cash available (the life insurance proceeds) to pay any estate taxes that are due as a result of your death BUT, if IRS guidelines have been carefully followed, the proceeds are not counted as part of your estate. (If you own the policy yourself, the proceeds just enlarge your estate, with the result that more death taxes are due!)

Estate planning professionals currently are looking at another way to accomplish this result, but the life insurance trust has been the workhorse in this area for quite a while.

Unit 8 covers estate (death) taxes in detail, so you might want to come back to this section later. If you find that even two estate tax exemptions will not cover your whole estate, you will want to remember that preserving two exemptions is not the end of what good estate planning can do for you.

C. "Living" Trust

The word "living" in the phrase "revocable living trust" means this is something you bring to life while you are living. In other words, WHAT IS LIVING ABOUT YOUR "LIVING" TRUST IS YOU![6]

Remember, each place I just say "trust" in this book, I am referring to a living trust—a revocable living trust.

There is a kind of trust that does not come to life until your death. That kind of trust is part of a Will and is called a "testamentary" trust. The estate must first go through probate; *then* it is transferred to the trust.

Two major advantages of the living trust over the testamentary trust are:

1. The property held in a living trust avoids probate. Property to be held in a testamentary trust will have to go through probate first, <u>even in cases where probate would not otherwise have been required!</u> In California, for instance, no probate is required for property that is passing to a surviving spouse...**unless there is a testamentary trust.** Then probate is required anyway.

> **Marie's husband, Al, had died almost six months before I met Marie. About a year and a half before that, she and Al had gone to two different attorneys. They had told the attorneys they understood they could avoid probate with a trust. The attorneys both con-**

[6]Sometimes you will see this called an "inter vivos" trust; that is Latin, meaning "among the living."

firmed that this was true and each gave assurance he could handle this for them. Al and Marie chose Richard, one of the attorneys, and he went to work.

Richard drafted a trust for Marie and Al...and then he tucked it right into their new Wills. Marie and Al signed their new Wills believing everything was handled. After all, they had a trust now.

Not until Al died did Marie learn the truth about their trust. She was worse off with it than she would have been without it.

In states where no probate is required for assets passing to a surviving spouse, Al's assets would have bypassed probate even without a trust. Now, since theirs was a testamentary trust, she had to put Al's half of their estate through probate.

2. The living trust is an asset to you during your own lifetime. If you were to become incapacitated, have a stroke or get Alzheimer's, for instance, the successor you had named for yourself could just step in and take over for you. No court conservatorship would be necessary for your estate to go on functioning.

Or let's say you decided to go on an extended vacation. Instead of having to make a lot of arrangements for someone to pay your bills, collect from your investments, deposit your checks, respond to your phone messages, mail and so forth, you could just hand your chosen "stand-in"—your successor trustee— the "keys to your kingdom" and take off.

Lesson 2 ■■■■■■■■■■■■■■■■■■■■■■■■■■■■

What Is A Trustee?

Because a trust is just a paper person, it will need a human person to act for it—to transact its business, to manage the assets it holds. That human person is called its trustee.

My files show that the great majority of people name themselves to serve as their own trustee. If you are handling your own financial affairs now, moving your assets into trust is no reason to stop. It is purely a matter of your own personal choice.

The name of the trustee is woven right into the basket that is your trust. So are names of successor trustees—people to take over when you want or need them to.

More than one person at a time can serve as trustee. For instance, if you are a couple, you may want to serve together as co-trustees. Parents sometimes name all their children to serve together as successor co-trustees.

Anytime more than one is named to serve at once, you should indicate whether the group must unanimously agree before any action can be taken or whether the majority may control. Interestingly enough, the choice that may seem more likely to assure that everyone has a "say" in the matter (requiring unanimity) actually puts any *one* of them in control.

The trustee is like a property manager. The trustee finds good tenants, evicts bad ones, collects rent, arranges repairs and so forth. A property manager (trustee) does NOT have the right either to live there herself or to keep the rent money for herself. That right—the right to use and enjoy the property—belongs to the beneficiary.

Managing our own property, our investments, our financial affairs is usually just so much a part of our day-to-day living that we don't distinguish between managing our assets and using them. These *are* separate activities though.

You recognize, for instance, that driving your car and deciding whether or not to buy a new one are distinctly different processes.

It will soon be clear to you that nothing new has been added. You have been playing both of these roles, wearing both hats, all along. (See Illustration 6-2) You just never had distinguished between them AND YOU WON'T HAVE TO NOW. In day-to-day life you will just go on doing what you have always done!

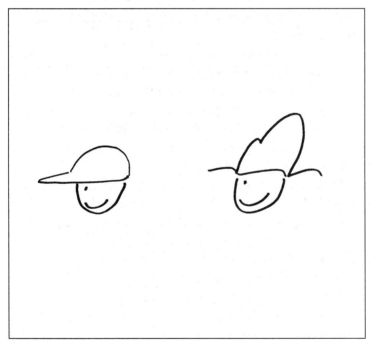

Illustration 6-2

Lesson 3 ▬▬▬▬▬▬▬▬▬▬▬▬▬▬▬▬

How A Trust Is Created

Like real baskets, trusts are sold in a wide variety of markets. Also like real baskets, they vary greatly in style, material, workmanship and cost.

I have seen one-page, pre-printed forms claiming to be trusts. I have seen a Will that declared itself to be a living trust. (This is not possible.) I have seen attorney-drafted trusts that were no better than ones prepared by bookkeepers, tax preparers, insurance salespeople, real estate agents, notaries, paralegals and others whose enthusiasm for their work is not dampened by their lack of training, experience or competence in drafting proper living trusts!

Having seen what people have brought to me asking for a "review," I have to tell you this: if you want to rest assured that your trust "basket" has been properly "woven," you must go to an attorney—an estate planning attorney.

Law has become as specialized as medicine. You may not have noticed, but few are general practitioners anymore.

I will have more to say about who should "weave your basket" in Lesson 11 of this Unit. *Whoever* weaves it, this basket gets woven with reeds made of words—*your* words. These are words that express your preferences about who gets what, when and under what conditions and who will make decisions when you can't any longer.

The resulting document is called a "trust agreement" or a "declaration of trust." When you sign it (some states call the person creating the trust the "Settlor," some, the "Grantor," and some, the "Trustor"), you actually create an independent entity, a "person" separate from yourself in important ways. A trust is not unlike a corporation in this sense, except that a corporation files its own tax return and your revocable trust does not.

Your trust will have its own name (e.g., The Karen

Johnson Family Trust, The Airedale Trust) and its own birthdate (the date you sign it).

Your trust will not need its own social security or tax identification number. As long as you are alive, the trust will use yours.

Lesson 4 ━━━━━━━━━━━━━━━━━━━━

How A Trust Avoids Probate

Here is how a trust works.

Once it is created by signing your trust agreement, the next step is to transfer your property to it. The mechanics of this are discussed in Lesson 9.

For now, think of gathering up all of your apples—the red ones, green ones, sweet ones and tart ones, large ones and small ones—and putting them all into a basket.

Illustration 6-3

The law rewards you for gathering up all your apples and putting someone else in charge of them before you died. It rewards you by allowing that someone to carry out your desires and directions independently, free of any supervision by the court.

If you had left your apples scattered all over, the court would have stepped in to see that they were gathered up, and then it would have stayed to oversee the rest of the process. This is just how the law of estates works.

It's not that our courts *want* to interfere or to create work for attorneys. It's just that, unless you have taken the matter into your own hands, the court determines you have left the matter in *its* hands, and it takes its charge very seriously.

Lesson 5

Trusts Are Not New

Trusts are being publicized so much these days that you may think they are something new. They are not. The law of trusts came over with the colonists from England. Every one of the fifty states has laws relative to trusts. A trust created in one state will be recognized by every other state, as well as by many other nations.

Why, then, is so much suddenly being said about trusts? Nothing for hundreds of years, then all of a sudden everywhere you turn it's living trusts this and living trusts that, replete with seminars, books, coupons, automatic dialings, door-to-door salespeople and direct mailings.

There are several reasons for this, including one that does not reflect well on attorneys in our country.

Lawyers have traditionally viewed probate as their "guaranteed retirement annuity program," as quoted in the January 1989 issue of prestigious *California Lawyer* magazine. This being the case, there has been an understandable reluctance by attorneys to get the word out about trusts. Renegades like myself are chipping away at this, but it is not being given up without a fight. A client of mine sent me a letter he received from his former attorney that addressed the issue of living trusts. It is twelve single-spaced pages presenting "reasons" why probate is better than a trust. Wow!?!

Another reason is inflation. Even if you still own just about the same assets you owned ten or even five years ago, you are "worth" a lot more today.

That house you bought six years ago, have you had it appraised lately? Have you seen the prices neighbors are getting for their homes? And, while almost all types of investments have their ups and downs, it is highly probable that your investments as a whole are worth more now than even five years ago.

The point is this: when the charge for services is a percentage of the value of the assets involved, the charge goes up as the market value rises, even though your assets seem like the "same old stuff" to you.

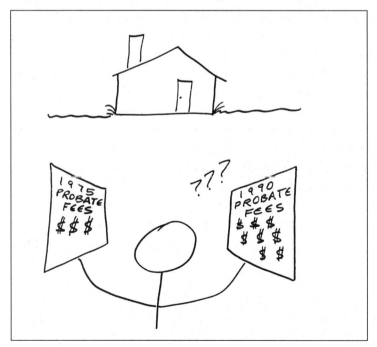

Illustration 6-4

Many of my clients have found that the cash it would take to probate just their home today would be more than the cash they needed to buy it originally! The same assets that might have cost hundreds of dollars to probate only a few years ago will cost thousands of dollars to probate today.

So, there is nothing new about trusts but your interest in them!

Lesson 6

The Difference Between You Now And You With A Trust

Look back at the picture of the people holding apples in Lesson 1. You can see that the person holding his apple in the basket is still in full control of his apple. Let's say that is you. You could remove the apple from the basket as quickly as you could remove it from your other hand. Nothing stands between you and your apple either way.

You can continue just to hold it, or you can eat it, bake it or juice it. You can trade it, give it away or throw it away. You can put other apples in with it. The apple can be golden delicious or made of gold—it does not matter to the basket.

If your basket has been properly woven, you will find that *anything* you could do with or to the apple before you put it into the basket, you can still do after.

Let's say that, instead of an apple, you have 100 shares of General Motors stock, and you put them into your basket (trust). You can still do anything you want to with this stock. You can keep it, you can sell it or trade it, use it as collateral for a loan, give it away or add more to it. And it is no harder to do nor will it take any longer to do than it would have before you put it into your trust.

In fact, nothing will be very different until you become incompetent or die. Then the apple you still hold in your hand will have to make its way through a costly and bruising court process (probate) where its survival intact is highly unlikely.

On the other hand, if you have put your apples into a basket, you simply hand the basket to someone you trust and all your apples go with it. No court processes are required.

Except for avoiding probate when you die and avoiding a conservatorship of your estate if you become incompetent, your revocable living trust is transparent in your life. It does not affect your day-to-day living any more than the way you are currently holding title to your assets affects your day-to-day living now.

Lesson 7

Who Doesn't Need A Trust

First, let me say that there is hardly anyone who would not be better off with a trust. To say it another way: almost everyone would be better off with a trust.

You may have discovered that your estate is so small, it would be exempt from probate in your state. Very well, but what if you become incompetent? There is no state I know of that exempts an estate, however small it may be, from a court conservatorship (called a "guardianship" in some states) if the person becomes unable to manage his own affairs—banking, paying bills and so forth—unless the person made other arrangements ahead of the need, such as creating a living trust or at least signing "durable" powers of attorney (the subject of Unit 10).

Or you may say, "My estate is very simple: it's all cash. My two children are to split my estate equally, and they will be my co-executors. Why would I need a trust?"

I have not been very clear if you think that the cost, delay and hassle I have described are only experienced by "complicated" estates. Complicated estates cost *more* and take *longer*. That is the only difference.

The fees you calculated on the **Probate Fee Worksheet** are where probate fees *begin*. Those are the fees for "ordinary" services needed by "simple" estates. A "complicated" estate will call for "extraordinary" services. Those cost extra.

A "simple" estate will require the minimum number of court hearings. A "complicated" estate, in which assets may have to be sold or in which beneficiaries (or creditors) have competing claims, will require more hearings and therefore will take longer.

You may say, "Well, I can certainly see how a large estate would save a lot of money, but mine's not really *that* large."

THE SMALLER THE ESTATE, THE LARGER THE SAVINGS ON A PERCENTAGE BASIS. The smallest estate that would have to be probated in California today would be $61,000 in gross value. Probate fees would be $3,960, or 6.5 percent of that estate. A $1,000,000 estate would cost $43,000 to probate. That's 4.3 percent of the estate. As you can see, the smaller estate costs half again as much!

It could be said that the *smaller* your estate, the *more* you need to avoid probate. The estates of the "rich," after all, may be more able to afford legal fees, bonds and so forth, while the "poor" need to maximize what is preserved for their beneficiaries.

Each person must assess her own circumstances, of course. It is definitely possible that the person with the $61,000 estate simply cannot spare the cost of creating a living trust now, no matter how much it might save later. (This is something to bear in mind if your parents have a small estate. They may be more interested in hearing about the trust if you offer to pay for it.)

When all is said and done, there may be just one group of people who don't need a trust: those who have named their attorney as their sole beneficiary!

Lesson 8 ▬▬▬▬▬▬▬▬▬▬▬▬▬▬

Selecting Your Trustee

If you are like most people, you will select yourself to be your own trustee. But you will need to name at least one trustee other than yourself. This is the one you want to take over when you (or both of you) are no longer willing and able to do it. This is called your successor trustee.

In selecting your successor trustee, one factor to look at is how long your trust will survive you. If everything in your trust will be distributed immediately after your death, then you will need someone to wind up your financial affairs, divide the assets if necessary, and distribute them to the beneficiaries you have named. You'll need someone who is conscientious, willing and available.

Incidentally, the "winding up" part consists of some of the same tasks that probate would have required. Your final income taxes must still be calculated and paid. Estate taxes may have to be calculated and paid. Your creditors must be paid.

Bypassing probate does not mean those things do not have to be done. They just don't have to take as long or cost as much as probate.

I would say that the least amount of time a probate could possibly take would be six months. I have seen trust estates brought to an end in three weeks. This is not to say that all or even most of them can be concluded that quickly, but at least this way it's not impossible!

If your trust will live on after you until someone reaches a certain age or some condition occurs, then, in addition to willingness, conscientiousness and availability, you may want to consider such matters as age, state of health, status of relationship, physical proximity to your beneficiary and temperament when selecting your successor trustee. After all, your trustee does not need to be a financial wizard herself, as long as you could count on her to seek advisors.

When your trust lives on, there are some additional parts to the trustee's job. That's why the trustee needs a few more "qualifications."

She will need to evaluate how the trust's assets should be invested while considering the purposes of your trust. Is income more important than growth or vice versa? What should be liquidated when cash is needed? When should distributions be made?

Finally, and probably most important of all, the person you select to be your successor trustee must, above all, be someone who has your total confidence—yes, someone you TRUST!

Remember, this is not a question of bringing yourself to ask someone to do this for you. Or of just skipping it because you can't possibly decide whom to ask. Someone WILL do it. Someone will have to do it. It will be someone you choose or someone the court chooses. If it's the latter, she'll have to do it the hard way.

Lesson 9 ▬▬▬▬▬▬▬▬▬▬▬▬▬▬▬▬▬▬▬▬▬
Putting Assets Into Your Trust

I have heard it estimated that only 1 in 1,000 of all trusts signed in our nation have any assets in them. This is an alarming statistic because A TRUST IS NO BETTER THAN A WILL UNLESS YOU MOVE YOUR ASSETS INTO IT. Anything not in the basket when the basket gets passed simply does not get passed in the basket!

How assets are placed into your trust depends upon what kind of assets they are. Some are handled with deeds, some with assignments, some with letters.

In this Lesson are examples showing how certain types of assets are transferred. This is not meant to be a "how-to" on transferring your property into trust. It is simply meant to give you an overview—to help you see how "non-exotic" a matter this truly is.

First, a word about "schedules." Sometimes clients who come in to confer with me have been told that, by merely listing their property on a schedule attached to the back of their trust, they have done all that is needed to transfer their property into trust. This is incorrect.

A schedule can be useful as a kind of inventory of your property or to distinguish between separate and co-owned assets. But a schedule does not *transfer* your assets.

Let's see what *does* accomplish the transfer.

A. Real Estate:

Anytime you are changing who owns a piece of real estate the transaction is best handled by a deed. This change in ownership from you to your trust is no different. It is best handled by a deed.

No particular form of deed is required. It can be a Quitclaim Deed or a Grant Deed or an actual Trust Transfer Deed. The latter has some things already printed on it that don't have to be typed on later; that's why I prefer it. But any of them will do the job. The top of a sample Trust Transfer Deed is duplicated in Illustration 6-5.

The language used can vary, but essentially the deed must show that you—with your name(s) appearing exactly as on the last recorded deed to this property—are granting (transferring) the property to yourselves AS TRUSTEES.

See Illustration 6-5 where Charles Clark and Mary Louise Clark grant to Charles Clark and Mary Lou Clark, trustees or successors, U/T/A dated 1/15/91. "Mary Louise" is how Mary Lou's name was entered on the deed when they purchased the property, so that is how it must appear first on the new deed. Since she uses "Mary Lou" as her name, that preference is reflected in how she is named as trustee.

Whose name appears first is your personal choice.

Transferring title to someone as trustee or trustees is how the transfer into trust happens.

Trust Transfer Deed

TTD 879 IA   THIS FORM FURNISHED BY TRUSTORS SECURITY SERVICE   181019

Grant Deed (Excluded from Reappraisal Under Proposition 13, I.e., Calif. Const. Art 13A§1 et. seq.)

The undersigned Grantor (s) declare (s) under penalty of perjury that the following is true and correct:
THERE IS NO CONSIDERATION FOR THIS TRANSFER.

Documentary transfer tax is $ _____ .
☐ Computed on full value of property conveyed, or ☐ computed on full value less value of liens and encumbrances remaining at time of sale or transfer.
☒ There is no Documentary transfer tax due. (state reason and give Code § or Ordinance number) _____
    Transfer to trust, not pursuant to sale.
☐ Unincorporated area: ☐ City of _____ and
This is a Trust Transfer under §62 of the Revenue and Taxation Code and Grantor(s) has (have) checked the applicable exclusion:
☒ Transfer to a revocable trust;
  ☐ Transfer to a short-term trust not exceeding 12 years with trustor holding the reversion;
  ☐ Transfer to a trust where the trustor or the trustor's spouse is the sole beneficiary;
  ☐ Change of trustee holding title;
  ☐ Transfer from trust to trustor or trustor's spouse where prior transfer to trust was excluded from reappraisal and for a valuable consideration, receipt of which is acknowledged.
  ☐ Other: _____

GRANTOR(S): Charles Clark and Mary Louise Clark
hereby **GRANT(S) to** Charles Clark and Mary Lou Clark, Trustees or Successors
U/T/A dated January 15, 1991

the following described real property in the
County of _____ . State of California:

---

consideration, receipt of which is acknowledged.
☐ Other: _____

GRANTOR(S): Charles Clark and Mary Louise Clark
hereby **GRANT(S) to** Charles Clark and Mary Lou Clark, Trustees or Successors
U/T/A dated January 15, 1991

the following described real property in the

Dated _____   Charles Clark

State of California

County of _____   Mary Louise Clark
On _____
before me, _____

personally appeared _____
personally known to me (or proved to me on the basis of satisfactory evidence) to be the person(s) whose name(s) is/are subscribed to the within instrument and acknowledged to me that he/she/they executed the same in his/her/their authorized capacity(ies), and that by his/her/their signature(s) on the instrument the person(s), or the entity upon behalf of which the person(s) acted, executed the instrument.

WITNESS my hand and official seal.

Signature _____

(This area for official notarial seal)

Title Order No. _____   Escrow, Loan or Attorney File No. _____

MAIL TAX STATEMENTS AS DIRECTED ABOVE

Illustration 6-5

"Or successors" shows Charles and Mary Lou's intent that whoever is serving as their trustee shall be treated as the owner of this property.

"U/T/A" means "Under Trust Agreement." January 15, 1991, is the date they signed it, the date their trust was "born."

So here you see the Clarks moving title to their home from themselves to their trust.

Illustration 6-6

The Clarks' home should not be affected in any other way by this transfer. Again, this is merely a different way of holding the title to the property and does not actually make any change in who "owns" it.

The United States Supreme Court has ruled that your lender is not affected by this change and cannot "call" your note. Property taxes are not affected. You can still borrow against or refinance your property. (Sometimes people are asked to take their property out of trust just long enough to complete the transaction. There is no legal necessity of this. However, this is easily accomplished and causes no problem as long as you remember to put it back IN trust when the refinancing is finished.)

Homestead protection is still available on your home, even though it is in trust. And your once-in-a-lifetime exclusion of $125,000 of capital gain on the sale of your home after you turn 55 is still intact. In other words, nothing is lost and everything is gained.

When you are transferring your home, don't forget any other real estate you may own, including partial interests. When you sign a deed transferring into your trust your interest in the ski cabin co-owned with your brother and sister, the deed transfers just exactly what you own: your third. Your brother's third and your sister's third are unaffected.

If the real estate you are transferring is not your residence, some special rules apply. Ask your attorney for guidance on this.

B. Stocks and Bonds:

If your securities are held in a brokerage account, just adding "trustee" after your name on the account moves everything in the account into your trust.

"Bearer" bonds are unaffected by any of this because whoever "bears" the bond owns it.

To transfer stock certificates that bear your name, contact the transfer agent whose name appears on the certificate and ask that a new one be issued to you as trustee(s). He will send you instructions and the forms necessary to accomplish this. Do the same for non-bearer bonds.

C. Promissory Notes and Deeds of Trust:

When someone owes you money, the note she signed is an asset of yours and should be transferred into your trust by use of a document called an "assignment." (If you have not yet had the debtor sign a promissory note, this is a perfect time to get that "cleaned up.") You should instruct the debtor to make her check out hereafter to you as trustee.

If the note is secured by a deed of trust, that deed of trust should be assigned to your trust, and the assignment should be recorded.

D. Your Own Business:

If your business is incorporated, give your stock certificate to the corporation's secretary and ask him to issue a new one to you as trustee.[7] (If certificates have never been issued, this is a good time to clean that up, too.)

If your business is a partnership or a sole proprietorship, your attorney should prepare an assignment of your share of the assets of the business to you as trustee. As you may have noticed, debts are disregarded; they simply are not accounted for in this process. Debts never require probate; only assets do.

E. Bank Accounts, Credit Union Accounts, Certificates of Deposit, Mutual Funds:

Send or hand-deliver a letter to each financial institution, showing the numbers of all the accounts in your name there. Instruct them to transfer those accounts to you as trustee. Usually they will ask to see proof that your trust exists. Your attorney should prepare a "certification" for you to use. This way you will not have to give them a copy of your whole trust.

Sometimes it comes as a surprise to my clients to see how close to them this has been all along. The same form they used initially to open their savings account at the bank,

---

[7] S corporations require a little more; confer with your estate planning attorney prior to its transfer.

for example, may have given them the option of having it be a trust account!

F. Life Insurance; Retirement Plans And Accounts; Annuities; Deferred Compensation; Stock Option Plans:

Assets that let you name a beneficiary, such as life insurance and retirement accounts, do not themselves get transferred to your trust like your other assets. Instead, your trust should be named as a beneficiary of these assets.

As for life insurance, whether you are married or single, your trust should be named as the primary beneficiary. As for retirement accounts and plans, like IRAs, Keoghs, defined benefit and defined contribution plans, deferred compensation, annuities, stock option plans and any other assets where a beneficiary may be named, your trust should be named as the primary beneficiary only if you are unmarried.

If you are married, I recommend that you name your spouse as the primary beneficiary and name your trust as alternate or contingent beneficiary. The reason is this: some payout options after death are available only to a surviving spouse. If the payment option your spouse prefers at the time of your death is available to any beneficiary, then he can "disclaim" the gift, diverting it to the trust.

Of course, if your spouse does not survive you, your trust, as alternate beneficiary, will receive the gift on behalf of the beneficiaries you named in your trust.

The advantage of having your life insurance proceeds and retirement account assets paid into your trust is that the proceeds will benefit from the same good planning you did for all your other assets.

I recently prepared a trust for Emily, who is a widow. When Emily came to sign her documents, I asked her if she had asked her life insurance agent to send her a change of ben-

eficiary form as I had suggested? No, she said, she was just going to leave her insurance the way it was.

Emily had forgotten what she said when we were planning together for her trust: though all three of her children were adults now, one of them had no "money sense" at all. She had decided that his third of her estate would remain in trust until such time as his sisters believed he could wisely handle an inheritance.

To leave her three children as beneficiaries of her life insurance would be to disregard her fears about her son. By naming her trust as her beneficiary, the son's share of the life insurance proceeds will be safeguarded in trust along with his share of the rest of her estate.

Another reason for naming your trustee as beneficiary instead of naming individuals is that most of the beneficiary designation forms provided by life insurance companies contain a statement that, if any of the beneficiaries you have named do not survive you, the proceeds will be divided only among those of them who do survive you.

Maybe one out of fifty of my clients wants this result. The other forty-nine want any children of the now-deceased child to receive that child's share. But they had skipped reading the small print.

To change your beneficiary, you should mail or hand-deliver a letter of instruction showing the numbers of all policies or accounts. Ask that your beneficiaries be changed as shown. Expect to receive the company's own form for this purpose. Complete it promptly and return it with a request for confirmation that the change has been made.

By naming your trustee as the beneficiary, you will know for certain that your preferences will not be overridden by the small print on an insurance company's form.

So you see, everything you own, with the possible exception of "everyday" checking accounts and automobiles, should be gathered up and moved into the basket that is your trust. This process can take a little time and effort on your part, even with the assistance of your attorney, but it will save a *lot* of time, effort, money and hassle later on for your surviving beneficiaries.

Lesson 10 ▬▬▬▬▬▬▬▬▬▬

Taking Assets Out Of Your Trust

Your relationship with your assets is the same after they are in your trust as they were before. Your trust is just as neutral as that basket you used to gather up your apples in Lesson 4.

If someone wanted to buy an apple from you, you would hand them the apple and put their money in the basket...assuming you were willing to sell.

If you wanted to eat an apple, you would do so.

When more apples fell from your trees, you would add them to your basket.

The same is true for assets in your trust. If someone wanted to buy one of your assets and you were willing to sell, you would "hand" it to them and put their money into a trust account.

If you wanted to consume an asset—spend $4,000 on a vacation, for instance—you would simply do so, by writing checks on a trust bank account, brokerage account or money market fund. The checks can be written directly to the airline, for example. You do not need to first take the money out of trust and then write another check. (This is true unless you are taking something out of your trust so you can make a gift of it. According to recent tax court decisions, in that case you must first transfer it to yourself as an individual and *then* give it.)

Whenever your income exceeded your current needs, you would put the excess into a trust account or buy an asset in your name as trustee.

Until you either die or become incompetent, you will go about your business exactly as usual, except for adding "trustee" after your name.

Do you have to sign "trustee" every time you write a check? No. I have noticed some people like to have that printed on their checks and to sign that way. That's fine, but it's not necessary. The only place your trust must be identified as the owner of your accounts is on your contract with your bank, on that card you fill out when you open an account. What is printed on your checks and how you will sign them are for you to say.

Lesson 11 ∎∎∎∎∎∎∎∎∎∎∎∎∎∎∎∎∎∎∎∎∎

What A Trust Costs

I am always amazed when someone calls my office just to ask what I charge for a trust. I am not saying that cost should not be important to you. But the question suggests that all trusts are created equal, that the only way they might vary is in cost. This is definitely not so. Even among trusts drafted by attorneys there is a tremendous variation in quality.

Plymouths, Pontiacs and Porsches are all automobiles, but they are not all the same quality, and they do not cost the same. Likewise, one trust is *not* as good as another, and the cheapest is no more likely to be better—or even to be adequate—than the cheapest automobile.

Here in northern California there are few adults who have not gone wine-tasting in the Napa Valley. I remind people at my seminars of that experience. You sample several wines at each winery, you experience the differences among them, and ultimately you select your favorites.

A trust is not like wine. You don't get to "sample" several different ones. By the time you get to "taste" your trust, it is too late to make another choice: you have either become incompetent or you have died.

It's good to get referrals to a good attorney from people you know. This does not assure quality, but it is better than calling "cold." Before you see anyone, you might do a little more reading on living trusts. I recommend a book written by Henry Abts III entitled simply *The Living Trust.* Mr. Abts' book is more than a primer. He covers the subject in much detail and does a very good job of it.

Armed with some information you will be able to ask questions as well as assess the quality of the answers you are given.

One important question to ask is: what can you do for me besides draft a trust? If the answer is that he can sell you insurance or annuities or financial planning or actually anything other than legal advice and legal documents, you are in the wrong place.

Some non-lawyers know quite a lot about trusts, and some of them know a good one from a bad one. But drafting a trust is legal work and legal work is best done by lawyers. Also, only legal malpractice insurance insures you against loss due to "faulty" trust drafting. Something to consider.

Sally's father, Eric, had remarried after Sally's mother died. He and his new wife agreed they would keep their estates separate: his two children would get what he and their mother had accumulated, her three children would get what she and their father had accumulated.

They told this to the man who came to the door selling trusts, and he assured them that was no problem. He came back a few days later with a trust, which they signed.

Then Eric died.

Sally told me she couldn't understand the trust and asked me to help her interpret it. After I read it I saw the problem. Sally understood it perfectly—she was just unwilling to believe what it said.

It left everything to the new wife!

Sally had already called the phone number on the card the salesman left with Eric and his wife. The number was not in service.

Some will say I have a vested interest in recommending you work with an attorney on your living trust and, of course, I do.

The truth is I am also in the unique position of being able to see many trusts drafted by other people. They are brought to me by people who are uneasy enough to want to pay me to review the trust they bought cheap.

I can tell you from firsthand experience that you are fortunate if you get an adequate trust from an attorney, much less from a paralegal or other non-lawyer professional.

So, go to an estate planning attorney. Once there, ask what percentage of his practice is devoted to trust drafting and other estate planning matters. If it's not at least half, go elsewhere.

Then see whether or not you feel comfortable with this person. You will be discussing intimate personal and family matters. Would you feel comfortable doing that with this person? Does she listen to you? Does she seem to understand what you are saying?

Remember, you will be paying this person a considerable amount of money. The least you should expect is to be treated respectfully, and that includes being listened to.

James Thurber said, "It is better to know some of the questions than all of the answers." Measure your prospective attorney by this yardstick.

Although prices will vary tremendously from state to state and region to region, as a rule of thumb you can expect to purchase an attorney-drafted trust that is appropriate to you and your circumstances for anywhere between $500 and $2,500.

At the bottom of the range would be a trust for a single person whose affairs have no complications. This price should include the "pour-over" Will (see Questions following Lesson 12 for more about the Will).

At the upper end of the range would be a trust for a couple with assets worth more than double the amount that is exempt from estate taxes, currently $600,000. This too should include at least a "pour-over" Will for each of you.

The trust and a "pour-over" Will are not all a person needs to rest assured that her life and affairs are beyond the reach of probate court. What else you need will be discussed in Unit 10. This, however, gives you a "ball park" figure for the trust.

Lesson 12 ▬▬▬▬▬▬▬▬▬▬▬

Is The Trust *Really* Flawless?

In my introduction to this Unit, I called the living trust the "flawless alternative" to probate. This book would be less than complete if I did not acknowledge that the trust has a few flaws too.

While a trust will save your estate the expense of probate, that isn't an expense that will arise during your lifetime. A trust will cost you more than just a Will, so the savings will be realized in the future and enjoyed, not by you, but by your beneficiaries.

Another flaw is that it will take some time and effort on your part to get all your assets transferred into your trust. What I hear from clients is that the amount of time and energy is greatly over-estimated by attorneys who want to discourage trusts.

There is no denying, however, that if you create a trust, you will spend some time doing things you would not otherwise have to do. This is time you could have spent reading a good book or playing golf. After all, it's not you who will have to endure the probate process if you don't handle these transfers before you die!

A third flaw is that creditors' rights end sooner in a probate procedure than if the estate passes by way of a trust. Creditors' rights are cut off after four to six months in a probate, while they are not cut off until after twelve months on an estate passing in trust. So, in an estate where there are serious creditor problems, it might be more to the beneficiaries' advantage to have at least a part of your estate pass to them through probate.

Finally, the good news that assets passing in trust avoid probate becomes the bad news if your successor trustee suffers a lapse in integrity. If so, all your planning may be for naught. If your trustee keeps all your assets for herself rather than distributing them to the beneficiaries you named, your beneficiaries will have to sue her. This would defeat your whole plan.

Questions

Can a trust be contested like a Will can?

Yes, a trust can be contested. But a properly drafted trust can absolutely be counted on to withstand a contest. If you think about it, the very *existence* of the trust is evidence against one of the things a contestant would want to prove: incompetence. Creating a trust is not the act of an incompetent person. Also, recall that a trust does not have to be publicly recorded or filed anywhere. This can make it a very hard target to hit.

Do I have to see an attorney every time I buy something and want to put it into my trust?

Definitely not, unless it is drafted that way. Some trusts are drafted so that a schedule attached to the trust must be formally amended each time the assets change, but this is not legally necessary. In fact, it is not even a proper way to assure that assets have been put into trust. Lesson 9 discusses the proper ways to move your assets into your trust.

I purchased a new car a couple of years ago. Right there at the dealership, when the salesman was completing the paperwork required for state vehicle registration, I instructed him to put the word "trustee" after my name. When the state mailed me the registration, it showed that title to the car was held in my trust.

Are there any on-going expenses related to a living trust?

Yes, there are a few expenses to expect once you have a trust. If you want to change your trust in any way as time goes by, then you should contact your attorney and have him prepare an amendment for you. This is a document that makes very clear what part(s) are being revoked and what provisions, if any, shall replace them. Expect a charge for this.

If you discover that your trust was not well-drafted, then it needs to be replaced. A whole new "body" can be slipped into the old "skin." You should expect this kind of amendment to carry the same cost as a whole new trust because that is, in fact, what it is.

The Internal Revenue Code is constantly changing.

Ideally your attorney will notify you when a change affects your trust and suggest you authorize an amendment if one is appropriate. If your attorney does not follow-up with you in this way, then you should initiate contact with her at least every four to five years to ask if any amendments should be considered.

If your trust was created by two of you together, then when one dies, the survivor will want to contact his or her attorney to learn what action is appropriate. Even if your trust was created by you alone, your successor trustee will no doubt want to contact your attorney to ask for some guidance about what's next. The initial overview is often given at no charge. Beyond that, however, there will probably be fees for any services a professional is asked to perform, whether that be your attorney, accountant or financial consultant.

If your trust is one that splits into two at the time of the first death, two separate income tax returns will be filed each year thereafter: one for the survivor and one for the Decedent's Trust. The trust's return will not show any tax actually due when all its income was passed on through to the surviving settlor, but the return still must be filed. Thus, there will be the cost of an "extra" return.

These are the only occasions that commonly arise when you should expect anything like "on-going" expense associated with your trust.

Does all my property have to be put into my trust?

Whenever you leave an asset out of your trust, you risk that probate will be required. Only the property outside your trust would be subject to that probate. But your goal should be to avoid probate altogether.

Almost all states have a law stating that, as long as an estate does not exceed a particular dollar amount in value, no probate will be required. That varies from $10,000 to $60,000. Find out what the limit is in your state.

As a practical matter, I suggest to clients that they leave out of their trust any bank account that is primarily a "conduit" between them and the grocery store, the paper carrier, the utility company and so forth.

Also, automobiles usually do not have to be probated as long as nothing else has to be probated. So I suggest that my clients don't bother putting automobiles in trust until they are acquiring a new one. Take title as trustee at the time of your purchase.

This advice about cars does not apply, however, if you have an automobile that is more an asset than it is transportation, such as a "classic" 1956 Chevy. Or if your transportation car is an exceptionally expensive car, such as a Rolls Royce, or if you own an expensive motorhome, you would want to put those into your trust.

If you find that the title to your assets has *not* been transferred to your trust, let this be your "tip-off" that something is very wrong. Either your trust is not a "living" trust, but a testamentary trust (which may have made things worse, not better), or your trust *is* a living trust, but your property has not been transferred to it. This is a big problem in either case. Check it out.

Once I have my trust, do I still need a Will?

Even when you have your trust you still need a Will, but it serves a different purpose than a Will that stands alone.

It is always possible that something of yours will not be in your trust when you die. It could be that you forgot it or you just never got around to it or maybe it didn't come to you until after you died.

Several years ago I prepared a trust for Alex, a man who knew he was close to dying. He told me his aunt had died almost two years before and left him a gift of money. As it turned out, the probate of his aunt's estate did not close until after Alex died.

Here was an asset that Alex didn't have in his possession before he died, so he did not have the chance to put it into his trust.

This is what the Will that is companion to a trust handles. It gathers up any assets not in trust when you die and puts them into it. If those assets are worth more than the amount exempt from probate in your state, then they will not avoid probate like the assets in your trust. But at least they will end up there, controlled by the good planning incorporated into your trust.

This Will is commonly called a "pour-over" Will. I see it like this:

Illustration 6-7

If I have separate property, do I have to have a separate trust for it?

A "basket" woven to hold property owned by two people can hold the property they co-own as well as any property either one of them owns by himself. The separate property does NOT have to be converted to co-owned property in order for this to work either. It can keep its "character" as separate property.

If you have been wanting to change any of your separate property into property co-owned by the two of you, this is a perfect time to accomplish that, but it is not necessary.

If you put separate property into your trust, you can express entirely different distribution preferences for that property than for your share of the co-owned property, if you choose. I have had many clients who directed, for instance, that their separate property was to go directly to their children even if their spouse survived them. In this case, only their half of property co-owned with their spouse would be held for the survivor's use and benefit until his death.

It is also possible for the person with separate property to be the sole trustee of that property, while being a co-trustee of the co-owned property with his spouse/partner. This lets that person continue to make independent decisions about his separate property, if he wishes.

Another point: the couple does not *have to* co-own anything in order to have one trust for the two of them. An unmarried couple, for instance, is neither blessed nor burdened with presumptions in the law about whether their assets are co-owned or not. So it is possible that all of their assets could be separately owned by one or the other of them. This would not prevent them from having what I call a "joint trust."

Will I have to get a tax identification number for my trust?

As long as your trust is revocable, the only tax identification number you will need for it is your own Social Security number. All your income is still *your* income and you will still be taxed on it, even if the asset that generates the income is now held by your trust.

Your trust will not pay any income tax at all, either instead of you or in addition to you.

If your trust will live on after you (or one of you) die(s), it will need its own number at that time. The number is very easily and quickly obtained.

Will my debts still have to be paid if my estate bypasses probate?

Your revocable living trust does not shield your assets from your creditors, either while you are alive or after your death. Your beneficiaries will have the duty to pay your creditors, *up to* the amount inherited from you. Their own assets will never be at risk for your debts.

Your beneficiaries may be harder for your creditors to locate when your estate passes through the use of a trust, if in fact they can even be identified. But the fact remains that they are responsible for paying your debts.

You may recall from Unit 2 that the probate process usually requires creditors to present their claims within a certain period of time. If they wait too long, they are shut out forever.

Estates passing through trusts have historically had no "cut-off" period, but the California legislature recently passed a law limiting to twelve months the time period during which creditors may file claims against a trust estate. A few other states have done likewise and many others are now in the process of doing so.

Is any part of what I'll pay to have my trust drafted tax deductible?

That portion of what you pay for your trust that can be allocated to estate tax consultation can be deducted on your income tax return. This assumes, of course, that your trust is drafted by a professional who is qualified and licensed to give estate tax advice.

Does putting my assets into a trust give me any income tax benefits?

With or without a trust, your income is your income. So your income tax liability is the same either way. It's like the way having a fishing license does not give you the right to drive. It gives you the right to fish, but it has no influence at all on the highway patrol. What your revocable living trust can do for you is allow you to avoid probate court in the event of your becoming incapacitated or in the event of your death. As to your income taxes, it is totally neutral.

Do I have to go back to the attorney who drafted my Will to have her draft my trust?

Your attorney is your employee. If you don't like working with her for *any* reason, or even no reason at all, you can hire another one. Most U.S. communities have plenty to choose from, heaven knows!

This is true no matter what kind of case you bring: personal injury, drunk driving, divorce, estate planning, whatever. Your attorney doesn't return your calls? Fire her! Your attorney doesn't inspire your confidence? Fire him! You didn't marry him, after all—you hired him!

Anyway, the point is this: you don't ever "have to" hire any particular attorney. Even if the one who drafted your last Will kept the original (a self-serving act, by the way, often described to the client as a "service"), that has no bearing at all on whom you should hire to do your next legal work.

My wife is the beneficiary of my life insurance; she's also the sole beneficiary of our trust after I die. Why do I need to name my trustee as beneficiary of my life insurance instead of my wife?

First of all, you cannot be sure that your wife will survive you. Even if she does, she might be mentally incompetent at that time. Unless she had signed a durable power of attorney (discussed in detail in Unit 10), a conservatorship may be necessary, which means ending up in court after all. This is one reason why your trustee should be named beneficiary of your life insurance.

Another point is that, if your wife ends up needing long-term care, her assets will have to be "spent down" before she can qualify for Medicaid (called MediCal in California). The proceeds of your life insurance become her assets if they go to her outright. On the other hand, it may be possible to draft your trust in a way that will shelter this asset from spend down. This can only work if the proceeds are paid to your trustee.

By naming your trustee as the beneficiary of your life insurance, you are allowing the proceeds to benefit from all aspects of the planning you did when you designed your trust. For instance, your trust may direct that, if your wife doesn't survive you, all assets are to be retained in trust until your beneficiaries have all reached a certain age or graduated from college. Again, unless the proceeds of your life insurance flow through your trust, the directions in your trust will not apply to them.

Do I have to make an inventory of all my furniture and furnishings in order to put them into my trust?

Furniture and furnishings do not have to be inventoried nor do they have to be appraised before they can be transferred into your trust. It is enough for you to sign a statement that all such possessions, together with your clothing and other personal effects, tools, books and so forth are, by your so stating, thereby transferred.

If my assets are in my trust when I die, do they still have to be appraised then?

A value should always be established for assets that are being transferred to a new owner at someone's death. One reason is to determine if any death taxes are due. Another reason is to establish the new owner's "basis." Lesson 5 in Unit 3 gives the details on this, but here's the bottom line: when someone inherits an asset from you, they only have to subtract its value *at the time they inherited it*, (not what you paid for it), from the price at which they sell it in order to calculate their capital gains.

Ordinary "stuff," such as most furniture, furnishings, clothes and so forth, don't have to be appraised, but real estate and securities, always.

I have my daughters' names on my bank accounts so, in case of some emergency, they could get to my money without any problem. Will I have to remove their names in order to put these accounts into my trust?

Remember that you "gather" your bank accounts into your "basket" by putting the word "trustee" after your name. It does not matter what other names may be there too. This just affects how *your* name appears.

Do consider taking other people's names off your assets anyway, however. You may want to review Unit 3, Lesson 3. A simple solution to the access issue is signing a power of attorney, which you should do anyway. (Unit 10 is all about this.) This will give your daughters the same degree of access to your funds without simultaneously exposing your funds to your daughters' liabilities.

Can my trust be sued?

Your revocable trust is not likely to be sued because it is nothing apart from you. It is just holding things for you. Suing you includes it and everything in it.

If I move to another state will I have to have a new trust?

Just like any other basket you may own, your trust moves with you.

What If my trustee doesn't follow my instructions?

The possibility that you may not choose well when you name your trustee must be considered.

The fact that your assets can be given to your beneficiaries without court supervision means your assets can be given to someone else, including the trustee himself, when there is no court supervision. No court supervision means no court supervision, for better or for worse.

You have at least two simple options if this possibility worries you. One is to name two or more people to serve as co-trustees. Three or four could run amuck, of course, but I think they are more likely to check and balance each other.

Your second option is to name a professional fiduciary, bank or other financial institution. In my opinion, a financial institution should be considered only as a last resort. First of all, most financial institutions won't even look at a trust unless it holds more than a half million dollars worth of assets. Secondly, they usually base their fee on the value of the principal and not on any measure of their efforts, amount of income or increase in value of the principal.

Finally, an institution is not likely to establish a personal relationship with your beneficiaries, though a person's financial support is a very personal issue. There are exceptions, of course.

I suggest that, before you name an institution, you make a list of all family members, including their spouses and adult children. Then make a list of all your friends and other adults who may not be "friends," strictly speaking, but who are within your circle of contacts. This would include your minister, financial planner, bridge or golf partner and so on.

Before you name an institution, first eliminate everyone on these two lists.

To Summarize This Unit ▬▬▬▬

The revocable living trust is a device nearly as old as probate itself. It will allow your assets to pass to your beneficiaries without the expensive, lengthy, cumbersome and public process that is probate.

Your assets MUST be moved into your trust or probate will not be avoided after all. But once those transfers are accomplished, differences in your day-to-day activities will be non-existent.

You must look at more than cost in deciding who will draft your trust. By the time it is discovered that your "bargain" basket (trust) has holes in it, it will be too late to replace or even repair it because you will be either incompetent or dead. A poorly drafted trust is worse than no trust at all.

Lots of folks confuse bad management with destiny.

—Kin Hubbard

UNIT 7

Addressing Your Own
Special Circumstances

L iving trusts serve

everyone by avoiding probate. Additionally, as you will see

in Unit 9, trusts enable people with larger estates to minimize,

if not eliminate, estate taxes by preserving the estate tax

credit of the first to die.

Some people, however, want trusts even if they don't

care about avoiding probate or saving taxes. Those are

people who have what I call "special circumstances" in

their lives. Ten examples of special circumstances are

discussed in this Unit.

Lesson 1

The Young Family

Whether their children are now five or fifteen, parents almost unanimously seem to believe 18 is too young to receive an inheritance of any size. Nonetheless, without some good planning, that is precisely when they will receive it should you die before they turn 18.

Much preferable to a guardianship, far more flexible than a custodianship (discussed in Unit 1), is a trust. A children's trust usually takes one of two forms.

One is a trust that holds the family estate intact—even though mom and dad are both gone—until a certain time or event. This is commonly called a "family pot" trust. It allows the youngest to have just as much to draw from as the oldest had.

For example, if one of your children needs braces on his teeth, you don't contribute the same amount of money the braces will cost to separate accounts for each of your other children. And, when another child wants horseback riding lessons, you don't put an amount equal to that cost into each child's account. Instead you fund all the needs you can out of one big "pot," without worrying about each child getting an equal share.

A family pot trust I recently drafted holds the whole estate in one piece until the youngest graduates from college or reaches the age of 25. The older children can apply to the trustee for advances against their anticipated shares, and the trustee has full discretion to honor such requests or not. Otherwise, the only distributions will be to or for the benefit of the younger children—the ones who did not get through college before mom and dad died.

Only if there are assets left after all the children have had the same opportunity to receive a college education will any child get any more than that, and then they will split it equally. This approach appeals to parents of young children especially.

The second way in which a trust can provide for your children is to split the whole estate immediately into as many equal shares as there are children. Distributions can then be tied to particular ages or events or number of years since the death of the parent.

Looking at the last one first, one family had me draft their trust so their children will get some amount outright at the time of the death (unless they are minors), a portion of the balance on the fifth anniversary of the death and the balance on the tenth anniversary.

More common are distributions tied to age of the beneficiary. Recently a client of mine, a single woman, chose age 55 for distribution to her only child. "That's when she will be thinking about retirement," she said, "and will really need and appreciate something more than what she has been able to set aside."

Sometimes more than one age is chosen: one-third at age 25, half the balance at 30 and the rest at 35, for example.

Also common are distributions upon the occurrence of certain events, such as high school graduation or a need to buy a home or a business or a need for medical care which the child could not otherwise afford.

Most common of all are distributions tied to a combination of age and event. Examples are graduation from high school or age 18, graduation from college or age 24, completing post-graduate or professional study or age 30.

The common denominator here is that, whenever distributions are directed, they will NOT be all outright at 18. That's the difference the trust makes. It allows your children to be supported at a pace more like the one you might have kept had you lived longer.

A final note: another advantage of the trust for a young family is that if one of the parents dies, the other—being young —is likely to remarry. Your trust can be drafted to help assure that your children and not the new spouse or any "new" children benefit from your share of your estate.

Lesson 2 ▬▬▬▬▬▬▬▬▬

The Disabled Beneficiary

A trust is also the way to prevent your gift to your disabled child or grandchild[8] from merely creating hardship for him. Unless your gift is made *in trust*, it can disqualify him from any and all public benefits he may be receiving. Anyone who knows how long and involved the benefit application process can be knows it's not something anyone wants to experience more than once!

> **Recently a woman came in who had signed a new Will not long before. Knowing how much her retarded niece appreciated little "extras," she had left her a gift (a "token," she called it) of $5,000.**
>
> **"Does your niece receive any public benefits?" I asked.**
>
> **"Oh, I'm sure she does," she said. "Her mother certainly couldn't support her."**
>
> **I broke the news to this woman that her niece's receipt of this "token" would make her ineligible to receive the benefits. The (re)application process can take five or six months, though the "token" wouldn't support her for much more than two months.**
>
> **The attorney who had drafted her Will hadn't told her this.**

Being qualified to receive public funds is sometimes a prerequisite for receiving other benefits.

[8]This is not meant to suggest that any particular relationship is required; it is not.

A case that comes to my mind is a woman with Down's Syndrome, thirty-seven years old, who had lived in a home with others like her since she was very young. The outright gift her uncle had included for her in his Will not only would have caused her to lose her monthly income, it also would have forced her to move from what was, to her, home and family.

The gift for your disabled beneficiary must be in trust, *a particular kind of trust* called a "special needs" trust. It allows distributions ONLY for special needs, which are, by definition, only needs not paid for by any public benefit program. A gift from a special needs trust can be for a vacation, for a massage, for purchasing a gift for Mother's Day or for something that might seem more ordinary than "special" to you, such as dentistry.

If any public agency attempts to force distributions from the trust, the trustee can be authorized to terminate the trust by distributing all its assets directly to the next level of beneficiaries you named when you created the trust. Otherwise, the trust will terminate automatically when the disabled beneficiary dies. Again, the assets will go to the next beneficiaries you named.

An outright gift to a disabled person is more likely to punish than to please. You need to put your gift in a "special needs" trust.

Lesson 3 ▬▬▬▬▬▬▬▬▬▬▬▬▬▬▬▬▬▬▬▬

The Elderly Beneficiary

The special needs trust described in Lesson 2 is also the way to provide support for your parents or other elderly beneficiaries without disqualifying them from public assistance they may be receiving at the time of your gift.

If you make your gift to mom outright, she would just have to spend it and then reapply for the benefits she was receiving before your gift.

Even if qualifying for benefits is not an issue, an outright gift to an elder is just going to enlarge an estate that will, more sooner than later, be subject to probate, if not to estate taxes as well. Your gift in trust, on the other hand, can give the elder whatever financial support she needs or wants, without enlarging her estate at all. At the elder's death, whatever remains of the money held for her benefit goes to the next level of beneficiaries you named, without passing through the elder's estate at all.

Lesson 4 ▬▬▬▬▬▬▬▬▬▬

The Single Person

Most of what is written about trusts discusses why married couples should have one. There are many reasons for a single person to have a trust too.

A single person is every bit as interested as a married person in avoiding probate. The fact that she is not the spouse of the beneficiary she has named does not mean that the single person is any less desirous of avoiding the cost, delay and hassle of probate.

A single person can be just as desirous of protecting her privacy—privacy as to the extent of her estate and the value of it . . . and privacy as to her choice of beneficiaries.

Also, a single person can be equally interested in setting into place the "machinery" to have someone else manage her assets if she were to become incompetent. In fact, a single person needs that even more than a married person because, though not always legally sanctioned, spouses have traditionally been allowed to speak for each other in many situations. I know of no state's law that allows a non-spouse to take *any* action for someone else, even a parent for his child if his child is no longer a minor, without a power of attorney or a court order.

And then there is this: of all the couples in the world, one half of each couple will be a single person again in his or her lifetime, unless they die simultaneously.

A single person may be just as eager as a married person to preserve her estate tax credit for a second "level" of beneficiaries, too.

Benjamin, for instance, wanted his long-time friend Charles to have all the financial support he needed for as long as he (Charles) lived, but upon Charles' death, Benjamin wanted what had been "family wealth" to return to his family with as little erosion by estate taxes as possible. A trust was the only way to accomplish this. Some people are comfortable making an *outright* gift to a person who "knows what I want him to do with it." Others prefer the certainty that comes with having their preferences spelled out on paper. Remember this: the weakest ink is stronger than the best memory.

If Benjamin's gift to Charles had gone to him outright, would Charles have kept separate books accounting for the part of his estate that he had inherited from Benjamin? And would he have signed a Will or a trust that gave all that was left of his inheritance at the time of his death to Benjamin's family? It's hard to know, isn't it? No doubt the amount of time between Benjamin's death and Charles' death would affect the outcome too. The longer we have something, the more it feels like it belongs to us.

Finally, there is the bonus of estate tax savings. If Benjamin's gift had gone outright to Charles instead of in trust, every dollar over $600,000 would have been reduced by 37 percent or more.[9] This is true with or without a trust, but without a trust, *another* big bite would have been taken when Charles died.

So, you see there are also compelling reasons for a single person to have a trust.

[9]Estate taxes are discussed in detail in Unit 8.

Lesson 5 ▬▬▬▬▬▬▬▬▬▬▬▬▬▬▬▬

The Unmarried Couple

There are many possible reasons for a couple not marrying. It may be a religious issue. For example, one or both of them may have been married before and their church forbids remarriage, or they may have taken vows.

The reason may be financial. Perhaps one of them will lose a survivor's benefit that came as a result of the death of a previous spouse, or they do not want to lose one of their two $125,000 exclusions of gain on sale of a residence.

The reason may be legal. Maybe one or both of them are married to someone else, or perhaps they are a same-gender couple.

Here is a tangible, legally recognized way for all of these couples to blend their lives without the license.

You will recall from Unit 6 that a trust is created by an agreement, by a contract. Our society respects contracts and will enforce them regardless of how it may feel about the parties to it.

Just as wife and husband can have one trust for the two of them instead of one for each, an unmarried couple can have just one trust, also. I call it a "joint" trust. Their joint trust can hold the couple's separately owned assets as well as their co-owned assets the same way the trust for married couples does.

Privacy is often highly prized by couples who cannot marry. They may have been keeping their relationship secret for years.

Therefore, the privacy that will result from keeping their affairs out of the courthouse is sometimes reason enough *alone* for them to have a trust.

People not maritally coupled are less likely to have children as a result of their union, so the two of them are less likely to have the same "second-level" beneficiaries. This means that, without a trust, the beneficiaries of the first one to die may end up with nothing. The survivor will be free to leave everything to his children from an early marriage or to nieces and nephews or her favorite charity, omitting altogether the heirs of the first to die. On the other hand, with a trust, each individual may state who is to receive whatever may remain of his estate when the survivor of the two of them dies.

Death is not the only event that can trigger distribution to second-level beneficiaries. Your trust can be written so marriage—with or without the license—limits or totally ends the survivor's access to the assets of the first to die. (Re)marriage is just an example. It is the event second only to death that couples most frequently want addressed. Your trust can impose almost any conditions you want to place on distribution from your share.

A living trust, whether each has one or they together have one, can result in even more savings for an unmarried couple than for a married one. For instance, many states do not require a full probate of property when it passes to a surviving spouse. (See Unit 2, Lesson 2 to refresh your memory.) However, when your beneficiary is not legally your spouse, no such waiver exists. Without a trust, the estate of the first-to-die will have to be probated before it passes to the survivor and then probated again when the survivor dies.

A final reason why an unmarried couple may want a trust even more than a married couple is that a trust is harder to contest. Since it never gets publicly filed or recorded anywhere, it is a hard target to hit.

If an unmarried couple will sign a trust (two single trusts *or* a joint trust) and durable powers of attorney (the subject of Unit 10) drafted by an attorney just for them, not forms, they can claim for themselves many, if not most, of the benefits society bestows upon the married.

Lesson 6 ▬▬▬▬▬▬▬▬▬▬▬▬▬

The Second (Third, Fourth) Marriage

More and more often, the couples coming to see me have had marriages before the current one, often with children from those earlier marriages. Even if the current marriage produced children, I have noticed that a parent often wants part of what is theirs to go to those "prior" children.

Without a trust, if the person with the prior children is the first to die, she has no guarantee whatsoever that those prior children will receive anything at all.

With a trust it can be guaranteed.

In Unit 9, you will see how a couple's co-owned, but undivided, estate can be divided into two parts at the time of the first death in order to save estate taxes. There is another reason to make this division even if the estate is way below the taxable level. That reason is to set something aside for the prior children.

The assets that are set aside for the prior children can go to them immediately, if you choose, whether or not your spouse or partner survives you. Or those assets can be held for the benefit of the survivor as long as he lives or until he remarries, and then go to the prior children.

The more you want to guarantee something will be left for your second-level beneficiaries, the more you will need to place restrictions on the survivor's access to the assets. The more the survivor can have, the less assurance you have there will be something left when the survivor dies.

In any case, the *only way* you can be sure your beneficiaries will get anything at all if you die first is to leave in trust the gift to the beneficiary who precedes them.

Before leaving the subject of the role of the trust in the life of the twice-married person, I want to mention that the revocable living trust serves very well as a type of prenuptial agreement. Holding title to your assets in your "basket" creates just enough distance from you to help you keep them isolated from any property you acquire with your new spouse.

Lesson 7 ▬▬▬▬▬▬▬▬▬▬

The Meddlesome "Ex"

Ex-husbands and ex-wives can be a source of great irritation.

> I remember one couple in particular, Richard and Wanda. His "ex" was always calling: what about this? What about that? The questions had nothing to do with the child, Bridget, who was born during their marriage.

> When Richard lay dying, his "ex" started repeated calls to Wanda and, in fact, came to the house! Whose truck was that? How much life insurance was there? How much retirement account money? The questions were all ostensibly in Bridget's interest.

> Whether they were or not, they were ill-timed and intrusive. Wanda called me to ask how many of the "ex's" questions she had to answer.

> "None," I said.

> When Wanda stopped answering questions, the "ex" called me. I told her I was not at liberty to discuss any of that with her. Then came the letters from her attorney. His client wanted to see the Will. (Richard had died by then.)

The next letter said, "As you know, Richard's Will just puts everything into trust. I am surprised that you did not send a copy of the trust along with the Will, but we expect your immediate cooperation."

I filed it.

As it happens, the trust provides for the child after Wanda dies. Wanda and Bridget had grown very close and it was also Wanda's wish to provide for Bridget. In fact, Bridget, then sixteen years old, knew all of this because Wanda had told her.

I never heard again from the "ex" or her attorney. She will never know what Richard owned when he died or whether or not he provided for Bridget. Even when Wanda dies she won't know unless Bridget tells her.

Unlike a Will, a trust never gets publicly filed or recorded anywhere. For those who value their privacy, who want to keep their personal matters as confidential after their death as before, the trust is a must.

Lesson 8

The "Wicked" Son/Daughter-In-Law

A surprising number of people come in and ask something like this: "How can I keep it out of the hands of her spouse? It will be gone in no time if I don't."

Anytime a gift is made "outright," which is the only alternative to "in trust," the receiver of the gift can do anything at all with it she chooses, including giving it to her spouse. Unless your gift is in trust, you lose all control over it, forever.

The closest you can come to keeping your gift out of the spouse's hands is to give the gift in trust and direct many small distributions rather than one or a few large ones.

You can even authorize your trustee to withhold distributions altogether if he thinks that is appropriate. With some assets you could authorize your trustee to invest directly—buy a house, for example—and retain title to it in trust. In this way the benefit can be provided in a form that neither beneficiary nor spouse can reach.

Otherwise, having delayed distribution, all you can do is hope your beneficiary will grow either in wisdom or spine as the years pass or else divorce before the whole inheritance has been squandered. At the least, you will have delayed the pillaging!

Lesson 9

The "Disappointing" Child

Within just the last few years, there has been a great increase in the number of people who reveal that one of their children is a "substance abuser," as it's often called today: alcoholic or drug addicted. They don't want to write this child off. After all, maybe he'll straighten himself out. But they also do not want to write him in, as they fear he'd "blow" an inheritance in a week or two.

A trust is the perfect answer for this circumstance. They can leave him a gift, but withhold it unless and until he cleans up his life.

Here's how I drafted it for Jim and Cathy, who have four children between the ages of 45 and 56. Their 52 year old son Harold is addicted to "coke." The other three are doing fine. So I drafted their trust to split into four equal shares. Three of the shares will go outright.

The fourth share, Harold's, will remain in trust with the other three children serving as co-trustees. They will have full discretion over distributions to Harold. If he dies before he gets straightened out, whatever is left of his share will go directly to his children, now in their late 20s and early 30s.

On the other hand, if Harold seems to be recovering, the co-trustees can make several small distributions to see how Harold manages them and can finally distribute Harold's whole share to him if that seems appropriate. This way they can let a "wait and see" approach continue even after they are both gone.

Lesson 10

The "Spendthrift" Beneficiary

The beneficiary with hands like a sieve is similar to the "disappointing" child, discussed in Lesson 9. You do not trust her not to squander her inheritance.

There is a provision that can be written right into a trust that will protect the beneficiary against herself by preventing creditors from laying claim to any assets in her trust until and unless the assets are actually distributed outright to her. This will prevent the spendthrift beneficiary from borrowing against what she cannot reach directly.

It helps if that beneficiary does not become the trustee, or at least not the only trustee.

One client of mine solved her problem this way.

She totally trusts the judgment of her two grandchildren, the daughters of her only child. So she made them co-trustees with her child. Any distribution requires the agreement of at least two of the three of them. This probably wouldn't work in every family, giving children control over their mother, but in this one it seemed the perfect solution.

Most people have worked too hard to accumulate what they have. In fact, I find they often feel they have little enough to show for their lifetime's labors. This is a way to at least slow down, if not prevent, your children's dissipation of *your* estate!

To Summarize This Unit ▬▬▬▬▬

There are several different objectives that can be met with a trust even if you don't care about avoiding probate or minimizing estate taxes. A trust can support your children at a natural pace instead of with a lump sum. It can benefit your elderly or disabled beneficiary without disqualifying them from needed public support.

A single person has as many reasons as a married person to want a trust.

A trust can enable you to blend your lives in a tangible, legally recognized way without marriage. It can protect the inheritance of your children of a prior marriage and can prevent your "ex" from knowing your business.

A trust can help keep your child's inheritance out of the reach of his spouse and can keep your estate from supporting a beneficiary's addiction, including "spendaholism."

I'm proud to be paying taxes in the United States. However, I would be just as proud for half the money.

—Arthur Godfrey

UNIT 8

"Death Taxes"

E verybody knows about
income tax. The amount you pay is based upon the income
you received during the prior calendar year, and it's due by
April 15. In addition, your records can be examined (au-
dited) by government agents.

Not everybody knows, however, that income tax is just
one of several taxes our federal and state governments
collect from us. Two others you need to know about are the
"estate tax" and the "inheritance tax."

The information in this Unit and in Unit 9 gets a bit
complicated, like tax talk tends to do. If you find your eyes
glazing over, skip to Unit 10 to read about durable powers
of attorney. Come back to taxes later!

Lesson 1 ▰▰▰▰▰▰▰▰▰▰▰▰▰▰▰▰

What The "Death Taxes" Tax

It may surprise you to learn that your "right" to name who shall inherit your property when you die is not an inalienable right, but a right *granted by our government.*

Our government could direct that all property we own at death be delivered to itself. This is what has happened until very recently in the Soviet Union, for instance. Most people could not own property to begin with, but if they did, it was all confiscated by the government at their death.

In exchange for allowing us to name our own beneficiaries, our federal government collects a tax on our property as it changes hands. This is the "estate tax."

Our nation's highest tax, it is based on the size of your estate—your *net* estate. Unlike probate, at least with the estate tax you get to subtract your debts. But also unlike probate, life insurance proceeds and retirement account funds must be included.

Again, this is a tax on your exercise of your right to name beneficiaries other than the government or a qualified charity.

Your state government may collect a death tax too. It's called an inheritance tax. It is in addition to estate tax. This is a tax on your beneficiary's exercise of his right to receive an inheritance from you! The amount of the tax is based on the size of the individual's inheritance. The state where the beneficiary lives is the one that controls this.

As of December 1989, more than half of the fifty states collected inheritance tax from their residents.[10]

[10]As of December 1989, the 24 states that did *not* have an inheritance tax were: Alabama, Alaska, Arizona, Arkansas, California, Colorado, Florida, Georgia, Hawaii, Idaho, Illinois, Maine, Minnesota, Missouri, Nevada, New Mexico, North Dakota, Oregon, Texas, Utah, Vermont, Washington, West Virginia and Wyoming.

Illustration 8-1

Estate taxes attach at point "A," where you direct what you own at death to the beneficiary of your choice.

Inheritance taxes attach at point "B," where your beneficiary receives the gift from you.

Lesson 2

Calculating The "Tentative" Estate Tax

To see how estate tax is calculated, please turn to the **Estate Tax Worksheet** on page 148 and we'll take it step by step.

First of all, you add up the fair market values of everything in the estate. Here you must include life insurance proceeds and retirement assets, unlike probate, which typically excludes these. Also unlike probate, however, you get to subtract all debts owed at the date of death. You may also subtract probate fees, funeral expenses and a few other items. What remains is called the "net taxable estate."

Let's look at a net taxable estate of $30,000; I'll call it Estate "A." Find the Federal Estate Tax Rates Chart on the following page. The tax will be found by using line 3 on the chart. The estate is more than $20,000 but not more than $40,000. Column 3 shows the "base" tax for this range, $3,800. To this must be added 22% of the amount over $20,000. Our $30,000 estate exceeds $20,000 by $10,000, so we multiply $10,000 by 22% and come up with $2,200. The $2,200 is added to the "base" tax of $3,800, for a total of $6,000. This is called the "tentative" tax.

Before considering what is meant by "tentative" tax, let's calculate estate tax for two more estates. First, Estate "B," $600,000. We will use line 10: the estate is more than $500,000 but not more than $750,000. Column 3 shows a "base" tax of $155,800, to which we must add 37% of the amount over $500,000, or 37% of $100,000, which is $37,000. $155,800 plus $37,000 is $192,800. So the "tentative" tax on our $600,000 Estate "B" is $192,800.

Finally let's take Estate "C," worth exactly $1,000,000. Line 11, column 3 gives us the "base" tax of $248,300 for an estate of more than $750,000. To this we must add 39% of $250,000 or $97,500 for a total tentative tax of $345,800 on Estate "C."

The amounts calculated so far are called the tentative taxes because another step is required before we arrive at the amount of tax that will actually be payable. The other step is to subtract from the tentative tax any deductions that can be taken (Lesson 3) and any credits the estate is due (Lesson 4).

Here is a chart showing the Federal Estate Tax rates:

CHART: Federal Estate Tax Rates

If the amount is:		Tentative tax is:		
Over	But not over	Base Tax +	%	of amt. over
$ 0	$ 10,000	$ 0	18	$ 0
10,000	20,000	1,800	20	10,000
20,000	40,000	3,800	22	20,000
40,000	60,000	8,200	24	40,000
60,000	80,000	13,000	26	60,000
80,000	100,000	18,200	28	80,000
100,000	150,000	23,800	30	100,000
150,000	250,000	38,800	32	150,000
250,000	500,000	70,800	34	250,000
500,000	750,000	155,800	37	500,000
750,000	1,000,000	248,300	39	750,000
1,000,000	1,250,000	345,800	41	1,000,000
1,250,000	1,500,000	448,300	43	1,250,000
1,500,000	2,000,000	555,800	45	1,500,000
2,000,000	2,500,000	780,800	49	2,000,000
2,500,000	3,000,000	1,025,800	53	2,000,000
3,000,000		1,290,800	55	

Lesson 3 ▬▬▬▬▬▬▬▬▬▬▬▬▬

The Marital Deduction

If you are married at the time of your death and leave everything you own to your spouse, there will be no estate tax due from your estate no matter how much it is worth. This is because there is an unlimited marital deduction.[11]

In other words, if your spouse survives you, there is NO LIMIT on the amount of assets you can pass to him FREE of estate tax. This means that if Estates A, B and C were all left to surviving spouses, there would be no estate taxes due on *any* one of them at the time of the first death.

"Well," you might say, "I'll just leave everything to my spouse. Then I don't need to worry any further about estate taxes."

The first problem with that strategy is you cannot be sure your spouse will survive you.

"If he doesn't," you say, "I'll just get married again, so I still don't need to worry about estate taxes!"

My experience is that, even when the surviving spouse marries again, she doesn't usually name her new spouse as sole beneficiary. She is more likely to be one who comes in to discuss a prenuptial property agreement. And remember, the marital deduction only "protects" the part of your estate that you leave to your spouse.

The truth is that, in any case, relying solely on the marital deduction to shield your assets from erosion by estate taxes is very poor planning. What you give outright to your spouse just increases her estate, making it that much more likely to be of a taxable size when she dies.

There is a way for you to make your assets available for your spouse if you die first, without just enlarging her estate. That is the subject of Unit 9.

Meanwhile, the point is that if your planning goes no further than the marital deduction, you really have done no planning at all.

[11]Special rules apply to non-U.S. citizen spouses.

Lesson 4 ▬▬▬▬▬▬▬▬▬▬▬▬▬▬▬▬▬

The "Unified" Credit

Turning from deductions to estate tax credits: at the time this is written, the Internal Revenue Code gives each of us a credit against estate taxes in the amount of $192,800. The relationship between you and your beneficiary is immaterial. In other words, this is not just for spouses or even just for spouses and children. This is a credit your estate gets no matter who your beneficiaries are or what their relationship to you may be.

Looking back now at Estates A, B and C you will see that the credit more than covers Estate A's liability of $6,000, so Estate A will owe no estate tax at all.

As for Estate C, from its tentative tax of $345,800 we subtract the credit of $192,800 and find that $153,000 will actually be due—still quite a lot, but not as much as it could have been! (And not as much as it will be if the credit is cut in half as was considered by the House Ways and Means Committee in 1990.)

Turning to Estate B, you see that the credit is *exactly* equal to the tentative tax: $192,800. Now you may understand why it is sometimes said we each have a $600,000 "exemption" from estate taxes. The credit ($192,800) covers the estate tax that would otherwise be due on a $600,000 estate.

By the way, this is called a "unified" credit because it applies to gifts you make during your lifetime as well as gifts you make at your death.

At this date, you can give up to $10,000 a year to as many people as you choose. Any annual gift in excess of $10,000 erodes your unified credit. For instance, if you give your grandson $25,000 (or assets worth that amount) to him for his twenty-first birthday, your credit is reduced by $15,000 to $585,000.

It is possible with a well-drafted trust to double your credit. This is the subject of Unit 9.

ESTATE TAX WORKSHEET

To estimate your potential estate tax liability, insert values of the following:

Your home	$ _____
Any other real estate	$ _____
Bank accounts and other cash assets	$ _____
Tangible personal property (furniture, furnishings, jewelry, collections and so forth)	$ _____
Securities (e.g., stocks, bonds)	$ _____
Your own business	$ _____
Amount of life insurance on your life (owned by you)	$ _____
Retirement assets, including any deferred compensation	$ _____
Any other assets (e.g., patents, mineral rights)	$ _____
TOTAL VALUE	$ _____
Subtract debts and charitable gifts	$< _____ >
Subtract funeral/administrative expenses	$< _____ >
NET TAXABLE ESTATE	$ _____
Calculate the tentative tax:	
Base tax on net value	$ _____
Plus ____ % of $ _____	$ _____
Total tentative tax	$ _____
Deduct the unified credit	$< **192,800** >
Deduct any available deductions	$< _____ >
ESTIMATED ESTATE TAX LIABILITY	$ _____

Note: The tax will always be -0- if everything is left to your spouse and your spouse survives you. This also assumes you did not use any of your credit on gifts prior to your death.

Questions ▬▬▬▬▬▬▬▬▬▬▬▬▬▬▬▬

I have heard there is also a gift tax.
How much is that?

Estate tax rates and gift tax rates are the same. In fact, the tax is officially called a "unified transfer tax" because it applies regardless of when you make your gifts, whether during your lifetime or upon your death.

As you read in Lesson 4, lifetime gifts will erode your credit if they exceed the $10,000-a-year gifts that are currently "free." Any such gift obligates you to file a gift tax return. No tax will be due as long as you still have credit left. But once you give away more than $600,000 during your lifetime (over and above the $10,000 annual gifts), you will owe tax on any additional gifts. And you will have no credit left to shield any gifts you make upon your death.

When are estate taxes due?

Estate taxes must be paid within nine months of the date of the death that triggers the transfer of assets.

What if probate isn't finished by the time estate taxes are due?

Probate, if required, will most probably not be finished by the time taxes are due. If there is not enough cash in the estate, assets will have to be sold to raise cash and that may require court action. This is an example of "extraordinary" service that can increase probate fees.

If money goes out the the estate to pay estate taxes, is it still included when probate fees are calculated?

Yes.

To Summarize This Unit ━━━━━

There are two kinds of death taxes. The federal estate tax taxes your exercise of your right to name your beneficiaries. It is based on the size of your net estate.

A state inheritance tax taxes the right of your beneficiary to receive your gift. States that collect this tax tie it to the size of the inheritance.

Estate tax goes as high as 55%. An unlimited marital deduction helps preserve the estate intact at the time of the first death, but relying on it can make the erosion worse at the time of the second death.

Each of us has a lifetime credit against estate and gift taxes worth $600,000. Good planning can allow a couple to pass up to $1,200,000 free of estate tax, thereby saving your beneficiaries as much as $235,000 in estate taxes. This is what a well-drafted trust can do for you.

Other strategies for reducing your estate tax liability are beyond the scope of this book. If you would like to explore this further, I urge you to make an appointment with an estate planning attorney or other estate planning professional in your community. Good planning can save your beneficiaries tens of thousands and, in some cases, hundreds of thousands of dollars.

Anyone may arrange his affairs so that his taxes shall be as low as possible. He is not bound to choose that pattern which best pays the treasury. There is not even a patriotic duty to increase one's taxes.

—Justice Learned Hand

UNIT 9

Saving Death Taxes
With Your Living Trust

A properly drafted trust can save a couple's beneficiaries as much as $235,000.

Here's how: If the couple's estate is worth exactly double the amount that is exempt from estate taxes — 2 x $600,000 or $1,200,000—and if this estate passes one half at a time, no estate tax will be due because each person has a credit that will cover $600,000.

If the whole estate passes outright to the survivor first, however, the exemption of the first to die is not preserved. Then only one exemption, the survivor's, will exist at the time of the second death. So his $600,000 would be sheltered, but the other $600,000 would not be.

Estate tax on that "extra" $600,000 would be $235,000.

By the way, it is not necessary for the couple to be married for this strategy to work. It is all in the way the trust is drafted.

Lesson 1 ▬▬▬▬▬▬▬▬▬▬▬

Cutting Your Estate In Half To Double Your Savings

Let's take a closer look at how this works.

Craig and Marilyn have a combined estate worth about $800,000. Let's say Craig dies first. Without a well-drafted trust, here's what will happen:

Craig and Marilyn's
combined estate
of $800,000;
each owns an
undivided half of it.

	C's assets	M's assets
	$400,000	$400,000

At Craig's death, all
that they owned together
will now be Marilyn's.

	M's assets
	$800,000

When Marilyn dies, there
will be only her exemption
to shelter the assets.

$600,000

The "extra" $200,000
will be taxed.

$74,500 TAX DUE

On the other hand, with a well-drafted trust Craig and Marilyn's whole estate could be passed along intact to their children or to any other beneficiaries with NO estate tax taken out. Here's how that works:

Craig and Marilyn's combined estate of $800,000; each owns an undivided half of it.	C's assets $400,000	M's assets $400,000

At Craig's death, his share of the estate keeps its identity as his; this preserves Craig's exemption.	C's assets $400,000	M's assets $400,000

When Marilyn dies, there will still be two exemptions to shelter the assets.	$600,000	$600,000

NO TAX DUE!

The names I use to distinguish between the trust holding Craig's share and the trust holding Marilyn's share are "Decedent's Trust" for the first (the share of the one who is deceased) and "Survivor's Trust" for the second (the share of the one who survives).

If you read other books on this subject, you will see many different names used. Examples are "credit shelter trust," "bypass trust" and "exemption trust." These all mean the Decedent's Trust. For the Survivor's Trust you will see "marital trust," "marital deduction trust" and "residual trust" used interchangeably.

Sometimes you will see these collectively called "A/B" Trusts.

At one of my seminars a woman shared that she read where the "A" stood for "above the ground" and "B" for "below the ground!"

Unfortunately, while some writers do use "A" to refer to the Survivor's Trust, others use it to refer to the Decedent's Trust. So much for memory aids!

I find it is easier for my clients to keep the two trusts straight with names that "tell it like it is."

Lesson 2 ▬▬▬▬▬▬▬▬

Dividing The Estate At The First Death

At the first death, all assets the couple owned together, as well as any assets owned separately by the now-deceased partner, need to be appraised. There are at least three reasons why these assets need to be appraised at this time. The survivor needs to know date-of-death values so:

1. She can establish her new "basis" (Lesson 5 in Unit 3 discussed this).

2. She will know whether or not an estate tax return must be filed.

3. She will know which asset or combination of assets will carry the "right" amount of value to the Decedent's Trust.

Provided that no more than the amount that was exempt from estate tax in the year of the decedent's death is allocated to the Decedent's Trust, no estate tax will be due on the assets in the Decedent's Trust when it terminates at the survivor's death. (Take a deep breath!) *This is true no matter how much the assets held in the Decedent's Trust are worth when the survivor dies.*

For example, let's say that Craig and Marilyn owned an apartment building worth $600,000 when Craig died. Marilyn could allocate that whole asset to the Decedent's Trust. That building could be worth $6,000,000 when Marilyn dies, and there will still be no estate tax on it at that time. As long as it was "covered" by Craig's exemption when he died, it will go tax-free to Craig's second level of beneficiaries when Marilyn dies.

I will leave to other books the "nuts and bolts" of splitting assets between the trusts upon the first death.

As the example of Craig and Marilyn suggests, it is often wise strategy to allocate assets likely to appreciate, such as real estate and stocks, to the Decedent's Trust, leaving cash and cash equivalents to the Survivor's Trust. This is wise, that is, as long as the couple's trust gives the survivor the full use and benefit of the assets allocated to the Decedent's Trust *and* as long as both persons' second level beneficiaries are the same. Otherwise an inequity could result.

I want to assure you that your trust can be drafted so the survivor will have absolutely *no loss* of control over the assets and *no loss* of any benefit of owning the assets (such as interest or dividends) so she can maintain the same standard of living regardless of whether a particular asset is allocated to the Decedent's Trust or to the Survivor's Trust.

The survivor can be the sole beneficiary and the sole trustee of both trusts. The result? The fox gets to guard the henhouse with the blessings of the IRS!

I would estimate that 80-85 percent of my clients elect to have me draft their trusts just this way, so that whoever is the survivor, he or she will continue to have not only full use and benefit, but also full control over all assets in the Decedent's Trust. (The survivor always has full use and control over all assets allocated to the Survivor's Trust, of course.)

In some situations a couple might CHOOSE to give the survivor less than full use or full control over all the assets. Or a couple might choose to give the survivor unlimited use and control, but only until the occurrence of a certain event, such as remarriage.

Your options are almost infinite. This is why it is so important for you to work with a qualified estate planning attorney, so you are made aware of your options and can make an informed choice among them.

Questions ▄▄▄▄▄▄▄▄▄▄▄▄▄▄▄▄▄▄▄▄▄

Will the survivor ever be able to sell an asset once it is allocated to the Decedent's Trust?

If the survivor is the sole trustee of the Decedent's Trust, he can make whatever changes he believes are necessary or appropriate in the form of the assets held in the Decedent's Trust. Let's say the neighborhood where Craig and Marilyn's apartment building (in Lesson 2) is located starts to deteriorate. Marilyn as surviving sole trustee has the power to sell it. Then she puts the proceeds of sale into the Decedent's Trust in the place of the apartment building. Later, if she comes across something that she believes will be a good investment, she can use the cash to buy it, and then it goes into the Decedent's Trust in the place of the cash.

The Decedent's Trust has its own assets. The assets can change form occasionally exactly as yours do right now.

Can the survivor even give away assets belonging to the Decedent's Trust?

If the survivor is sole trustee of the Decedent's Trust, he can make gifts of assets belonging to the Decedent's Trust if the trust agreement gives him that power. Because the assets in the Decedent's Trust are sheltered from estate tax, it might be better strategy for the trustee to exchange an asset in his Survivor's Trust for the asset held in the Decedent's Trust that he wants to give away, and then give it out of Survivor's Trust. This way the estate-tax-exempt estate remains intact.

Asset management decisions like this always require an analysis of the prevailing facts and circumstances. My intent is merely to give you a feeling for the amount of discretion the trustee can exercise.

So assets can be exchanged back and forth between the Decedent's Trust and the Survivor's Trust?

Yes, assets can be exchanged between the two trusts, as long as exchanges are made at then-current values. For example, let's say the trustee notices that an asset he allocated to his Survivor's Trust, let's call it "Asset A," is appreciating rapidly and he wants that appreciation to come under the estate-tax-sheltered Decedent's Trust. Well, it is too late for the appreciation that has already occurred, but he can exchange it for something already in the Decedent's Trust that is worth what "Asset A" is *now* worth. At least then any future appreciation will be sheltered.

What is a "QTIP" Trust?

"QTIP" stand for "qualified terminable interest property." A QTIP trust is one that qualifies for the marital deduction, so no estate taxes are due on the first death, but it does not give the surviving spouse control over who gets whatever assets remain in it when she dies.

This is useful where the deceased spouse's share of the

family estate exceeds his estate tax credit, so you would not want to put it all in the Decedent's Trust. The balance of his half could be placed in a QTIP Trust.

When a couple adds a QTIP Trust to their family trust, they will know that, no matter which one of them dies first, his beneficiary and not the survivor's will get whatever is left of his half of the family estate when the survivor dies.

Otherwise, without the QTIP Trust, the balance of the deceased spouse's half would either: (1) spill over into the Survivor's Trust where the survivor's beneficiaries would get whatever was left when the survivor dies or (2) be given outright to a third person or held in a non-QTIP Trust, in which case estate taxes would be immediately due and not deferred until the survivor's death.

Where both spouses name the same second level beneficiaries, the children of their marriage, for instance, the QTIP serves small purpose.

To consider the usefulness of strategies like this for your estate, I urge you to confer with an estate planning professional.

To Summarize This Unit ▬▬▬▬

If you are a couple and you have a trust that is well drafted, your beneficiaries can receive up to $235,000 more than they otherwise would have. This is because a trust can preserve *until the second death* the estate tax credit of the first to die. The division of the assets that is necessary to accomplish this does not have to mean the survivor will suffer loss of use, benefit or control.

May you live all the days of your life.
　　　　　　　　　　　　　　—Jonathan Swift

UNIT **10**

Is Living Longer Good For Your Health?
Or, Why You *Must* Have "Durable"
Powers Of Attorney

Our newspapers and magazines tell us we are living longer. The sad truth is that, because we are living longer, more of us may be incapacitated before we die.

If you do become incapacitated and are unable to handle your own financial affairs—make deposits, pay your bills on time and so forth—then someone else must do it for you. If you cannot make or express decisions about your health or personal care, someone else must do that for you.

Either the court will appoint that "someone" and he will be called your "conservator," *or* you can authorize someone ahead of time by signing "durable" powers of attorney.

In this Unit you will first learn about doing it the hard way: the conservatorship. Then you will learn about your alternatives.

Lesson 1 ▬▬▬▬▬▬▬▬▬▬▬▬▬▬

The Conservatorship

In Unit 2 I described probate as a "default setting." Probate is what happens when you die if you didn't plan something else.

A conservatorship is a default setting too. It is what happens if you become incapacitated and didn't plan for that to be handled outside the court system.

A conservatorship is a court process to appoint someone to represent you—to act on your behalf—if you become incapacitated.

A conservatorship is as invasive of your privacy as probate. An inventory of your whole estate must be filed with the court, together with an appraisal of each asset. An accounting must be filed by your conservator a year later showing all income received: what date, from whom, for what and how much, all disbursements made: what date, to whom, for what, how much, and any property on hand. Like probate files, conservatorship files are public records, open for the inspection of anyone who asks.

Some states require that an accounting be filed with the court every year. Some, like California, require an accounting every two years after the first one.

A conservatorship is actually *more* invasive than probate because incompetence can be harder to prove than death. Some states require that an investigator assigned by the court visit you and make a written report to the judge on his observations and impressions of you. This is in addition to whatever evidence of incompetence is being offered by the person seeking to be appointed your conservator.

Though intended to protect people, conservatorships can become part of the problem, stripping a person of her dignity as well as her privacy.

Conservatorships are not inexpensive either. Most people will hire an attorney rather than spend the time and effort to learn the process themselves. My experience suggests that at least five or six attorney hours will be consumed in explaining the process, gathering the necessary information and setting it out in the manner required by the court. Then there is the court appearance on the date the judge considers the petition. Allow at least one hour for that.

How much time will be required for the attorney to prepare the inventory and secure the appraisals varies, depending not so much on the size of the estate as on how it is held. Two million in real estate is usually easier to inventory than $200,000 of a little of this and a little of that. Allowing three to four hours for the inventory brings to about ten hours the total for initiating a conservatorship. Multiply by ten the usual hourly fee for attorney services in your community, and you will be very close to what a conservatorship will cost to establish.

How much easier, cheaper and more private it would be to name someone ahead of time to step into your shoes if you become incapacitated.

Can you do that?

Yes.

The revocable living trust is the best way to authorize your own successor. Let's say that, to start out, you (or you and your spouse) will be trustee(s) of your trust. Your trust will also name the person(s) or institution(s) to take over when you (or both of you) cannot function as trustee any longer because of either death or incompetence.

A well-drafted trust will specify within it what evidence can prove your successor's authority. The evidence may be a letter from your family physician or the written consensus of your children or your own request that your successor take over for you, for example.

Your trust can set forth something much more complex than that, if you prefer. I have a client who gave me a list of names of "category A" people: these were physicians, psychotherapists and her minister—and "category B" people: certain relatives and friends. There were to be statements from two people in category A and three people in category B.

Your trust could even require that a court had to declare you incompetent, but that would defeat one purpose of your trust: to keep your affairs OUT of court.

Nevertheless, the point is this: in your trust you have the opportunity to name your own successor and to specify for yourself what shall be the conditions of his taking over. Then, if those conditions are ever met, your successor steps in, picking up wherever you left off. There is no delay, no cost, no courthouse hassle.

Bear in mind that, just as you saw in my discussion of avoiding probate with a living trust, here, too, the trustee can only control what is IN your trust. If it is true that only 1 in 1,000 of the trusts people have signed are "funded," then they will be of little use should incompetence come too.

As with probate, any assets *not* in trust do *not* avoid the courthouse.

To be sure your objectives will be met by your estate planning documents, I recommend you sign a durable power of attorney at the same time you sign your trust. Then, any asset you do not transfer into your trust yourself before you become incapacitated, can still be transferred in by the person you name in your power of attorney. (This is usually the same person you named as your successor trustee.)

Leaving an asset out of trust is sometimes an oversight. "I just forgot all about it." Sometimes it is deliberate—the "everyday" checking account which never holds more than $3,000-$4,000. And sometimes it is unavoidable.

Only a few months ago I heard of a case where a whole conservatorship had to be established because of a car that was worth little more than the cost of the court procedure.

The reason?

The woman had a living trust. In fact, she had transferred all her property into it before she became incompetent. But her brother left her his automobile in his Will, and she became incompetent before the probate of his estate terminated!

So, you see, an asset could be left out of your trust even if you were sure to put "everything you own" into it. There was no way this car could have been put into this woman's trust before she became incompetent because she had not received it. A durable power of attorney would have prevented this silly result.

Lesson 2 ▬▬▬▬▬▬▬▬▬▬▬▬▬▬

The Financial "Durable" Power Of Attorney

"Power of attorney" is the name of the document you sign giving someone the power to take some action in your behalf. Let's say you have a car you want to sell, but you leave on vacation before selling it. You might give your brother your power of attorney authorizing him to sign all the necessary papers for you if he finds a buyer while you are away.

Now let's say you gave your brother your power of attorney because you realized you were mentally "slipping" and he offered to handle your affairs. A "regular" power of attorney would be ineffective because, just when it was needed—when you became incompetent—it would expire. That's the difference between durable powers of attorney and regular powers of attorney.

A durable power of attorney will be unaffected by your incompetence and it will say so, usually at the beginning of it. The documents I prepare state: "This power of attorney shall not be affected by incapacity of the principal." (The "principal" is the person signing the document—*you*, in other words.) This feature of durable powers of attorney makes them highly useful estate planning tools.

This subject of durable powers of attorney arose in the context of how you can avoid the necessity of a conservatorship just for a few assets left out of trust. But a durable power of attorney is just as useful where there is no trust. If *any* of your assets *are* in trust, at least those will not require a conservatorship. But, if you have no trust, *all* your assets will be out of trust, and a conservatorship will be required for all of them unless other planning has been done. That "other planning" can be a durable power of attorney.

When you have a trust, the agent you name in your durable power of attorney, if it is properly drafted, can bring your whole estate together in your trust and handle it as your trustee. When you do not have a trust, your agent will handle your whole estate under the powers you granted to him in your durable power of attorney. In either case, a costly and invasive conservatorship is avoided.

Lesson 3 ▬▬▬▬▬▬▬▬▬▬▬▬▬▬▬▬

The Health Care Durable Power Of Attorney

The durable power for your health care is where you put your preferences, directions and requests as to your health and personal care. I find that the foremost of those issues for most people is the "heroic measures" issue.

Almost every state now has what is called a "Natural Death Act," a law which gives legal force to a "Living Will." This is the name given to a document in which a person states that, if she should have an incurable injury, disease or illness, she wants life-sustaining procedures withheld *or* withdrawn if they would only "artificially prolong the moment of death." Enthusiastically received *in concept,* the Living Will has not been widely used.

These are some of the reasons for its limited use:

1. Living Wills only express the desire to have medical treatment terminated. They do not accommodate those who want to express any other preference *or* who want to address any circumstance other than incurable terminal disease, injury or illness.

2. The Living Wills set forth in most states' statutes use vague terminology, both as to the health conditions addressed and the treatments to be terminated. What really IS a "heroic measure," for instance? Some statutes restrict Living Wills to cases of terminal illness. At what point in time is an illness "terminal?" What about a vegetative state that is not the result of illness, terminal or otherwise?

3. Most Living Wills do not allow you to name someone to make decisions when you either cannot or at least are not able to express them.

The durable power of attorney for health care has none of these disadvantages. Dependent also upon the language skills of you and the drafter, your durable power for health care may also contain vague terminology. However, you can express a full range of preferences about your medical care, including ones that vary with the health conditions that might be presented. Many of my clients, for instance, want one type of treatment if they are terminally ill but another if they are in a coma diagnosed as irreversible.

The durable power allows you to name an agent to speak for you if you have become unable to speak for yourself. By choosing someone you trust and who knows you well, and by discussing your health care preferences with that person, you will come as close as possible to ensuring your wishes will be both expressed and respected if an illness or injury leaves you unable to make your own decisions.

Despite the fact that the typical durable power of attorney for health care drafted today has much room for linguistic improvement, it is still the most effective document of its kind in use today anywhere in the United States.

And, for expressing preferences about issues other than life-sustaining treatment, it is limitless. Disposal of remains, anatomical gifts, autopsy, care at home, nontraditional forms of treatment, organ transplants, services or celebrations, all these and more can be covered in the durable power of attorney for health care.

The conservatorship explored in Lesson 1 was a conservatorship "of the estate," which is necessary if you had signed neither a living trust nor a durable power of attorney empowering someone to handle your affairs.

There is also a conservatorship "of the person," called a "guardianship" in some states. There is no alternative to this unless you sign a durable power of attorney for your health care.

Questions

Can my trustee make medical decisions for me in an emergency?

Your trustee has no authority to make decisions having to do with your health or personal care.

You see, the law divides you into two parts: your person and your estate. Your trust only has to do with what you own, your estate. The durable power of attorney I discussed in Lesson 2, also only has to do with your estate.

To empower someone to make medical decisions for you, you must sign a durable power for your health care.

Who needs to sign a durable power of attorney for health care?

Anyone who is no longer a minor, 18 in most states, should sign a durable power of attorney for her health care. A parent can give medical consent for his child, but only until the child becomes an adult.

Don, an accountant I know, has a son, Michael, who went away to college a couple of years ago.

Two weeks into the school quarter, Don received a phone call from a hospital in the city where Michael had started college. Michael had been admitted there following a collision between an automobile and him on his bicycle. Could Don give them some information? Of course, he said. He would get there just as soon as he could.

One of the first things the hospital asked Don for when he arrived was Michael's Social Security number. He didn't have that, he said, but wasn't Michael carrying his wallet?

Yes, they said, he was and they had it, but they couldn't give it to Don. Since Michael was no longer a minor, they could not release his wallet to anyone without a power of attorney or a court order. It made no difference that Don was his father, they explained.

Don had to locate an attorney who could help him on such short notice, someone who could get him into court quickly to be appointed Michael's conservator. Only then could he claim Michael's wallet from the hospital so that he could give the information they wanted!

Needless to say, not until he had his conservator papers would he have any authority to consent to medical treatment, either. Don learned the harsh truth that neither parent (nor spouse) is invested with lifetime authority to consent or withhold consent to medical treatment of his child (or spouse). Traditionally, doctors and hospitals accepted the consent of a parent or spouse of a patient, but in these litigious times, this is definitely more the exception than the rule. You will need court authorization unless a durable power of attorney was signed.

To Summarize This Unit

The time for you to sign durable powers of attorney, *both* of them, is now. You carry car insurance even though you don't expect to be in an accident, and homeowner's insurance even though you don't expect your house to burn down. Signing a durable power of attorney is like carrying insurance; you do it so you'll have it if you do need it.

If you wait until you need it, you have waited too long!

Index